NOBODY'S PERFECT

Nobody's Perfect

How to Give Criticism and Get Results

DR. HENDRIE WEISINGER

and

NORMAN M. LOBSENZ

Published by

Stratford Press

LOS ANGELES

Distributed by
Harper & Row
NEW YORK

ISBN 0-936906-07-3
Library of Congress Catalog Card 81-52013

MANUFACTURED IN THE UNITED STATES OF AMERICA

FOR MY PARENTS—

My Most Constructive Critics

H.W.

Contents

Acknowledgments

It would be impossible to acknowledge all those whose work in the areas of interpersonal psychology and psychotherapy contributed to the basis of this book. However, there are a few individuals who deserve special mention:

Dr. Ronald M. Podell, for his comments and ideas pertaining to sexual criticism; Dr. Ian Fluger, for his insights on communication and the role of criticism in work; Dr. Darwin Eads, for his contributions to the criticism inventories used in my workshops; Richard B. Cohen, for his views on criticism as an interactive process and an engine of change; Dr. Ken Cinnamon, who first recognized the importance of criticism as an interpersonal skill and "demanded" that the book be written; Dr. Janos Kalla, for his encouragement to teach classes in criticism; Ms. Sally O'Neill, of the Extension Division of the University of California at Los Angeles, who gave me the opportunity to implement my work; and the psychology staff of the Brentwood Veterans Administration Hospital, who served as an encouraging source and resource.

My coauthor, Norman Lobsenz, had the difficult

task of sorting out my ideas, criticizing them, and significantly contributing to them so they would be communicated accurately and with impact.

Most of all, my wife, Lorie Beth, supplied me with love, energy and encouragement; without her devotion this book would not have been written.

H.W.

1 | Criticism Is Just a Four-Letter Word: Grow!

Does being criticized often leave you feeling angry, resentful, belittled or rejected? Do you at times make others feel that way, even unintentionally, by critical remarks? Do you hesitate to offer what you honestly believe would be helpful personal criticism for fear of offending someone?

For most people the answer to all of these questions is "Yes." True, there is the occasional individual who seems oblivious or impervious to criticism. But that requires a towering amount of self-assurance or a vastly overblown ego, such as that possessed by the actor whose performance in the title role of *Hamlet* was so abysmal that when he finished the "To be or not to be" soliloquy, the audience jeered. "It's no use booing me," he said, "I didn't write this stuff." Save for the few who are so insensitive as not even to recognize a critical remark when it is leveled at them, virtually everyone finds criticism difficult to accept and embarrassing to give. This is especially true

1

when the critic is a person important to our lives—a boss, a friend, a lover, a spouse.

The instant Ken sped past the freeway off-ramp he realized he had passed his exit. It would be another six miles before he could turn off and circle back. Ken hoped Eileen hadn't noticed, but when he heard the rustle of the road map he knew she was about to pounce on his mistake.

"Weren't we supposed to turn off back there?" she asked.

Ken nodded. "Must have been daydreaming. But the next exit is only a few minutes away."

"The trouble with you is, you never pay attention to road signs," Eileen said. "You're always getting us lost or making us late. Next time I'd better drive!" Ken knew there was no point in trying to answer his wife's sweeping rebuke. He swallowed his anger and drove on in silence.

———

Sally put her sketches for the new ad campaign on the art director's desk. Her boss flipped through them without a flicker of expression. They were good enough, but he knew she could do better. Besides, he didn't want Sally to think her first effort would be so quickly accepted. Brusquely he pushed the sketches back toward the young woman. "Do you want to try again, or should I give the job to someone else?"

Shamed and hurt, Sally fought to control her

feelings. "I'll try again," she said. She didn't break into tears until she had reached her own cubicle and shut the door.

———

When Pam had finished dressing for her big date, she asked her roommate how she looked. Carol knew that Pam's scarf clashed with her dress and that her shoes were absolutely wrong for the rest of the outfit, but Carol kept her opinions to herself. She did not even point out that Pam was wearing too much makeup. Carol knew from experience that her roommate resented any critical remarks about her appearance—even though she asked for them. "Why antagonize her when I have to live with her?" Carol thought. So, instead of being honestly helpful, she simply said, "You look fine, Pam."

The Axe of Criticism

Criticism produces the difficult situations and painful reactions seen in the preceding examples because people automatically tend either to use and interpret it in a totally negative way, or to refrain from criticizing for largely negative reasons. Were you to choose at random a hundred people and ask them to tell you what the word *criticism* meant, chances are they would overwhelmingly characterize it as an opinion or observation that is destructive, humiliating or hostile, the purpose of which is to find fault.

This popular concept derives from, and is supported by, the authority of experts. Most dictionaries define *criticize* as "to stress the faults of: cavil at." *Criticism* is said to be "the act of criticizing, usually unfavorably." The synonyms most often suggested for *criticize* include *blame, censure, condemn, denounce, reprehend.* No wonder the traditional image of criticism is that of a personal attack; no wonder most of us think of it as a hurtful comment about discreditable behavior.

We are so perversely attached to the idea that criticism isn't criticism unless it destroys something, that we scarcely notice the extent to which this damaging concept is carried. "Flaw-finding seems to be the most dominant, the traditional, and the expected response" to attempts at change or innovation, observes sociologist Stephanie Hughes, an expert in studying how people give and take criticism. According to Hughes, negative criticism is the standard technique by which most reviewers judge books and films, by which government agencies assess various options to reach their decisions, and by which business and industry evaluate products, procedures and personnel.[1] In short, most of those who see criticism as a tool seem to think of it only as an axe or a sledgehammer. It is hardly surprising, then, that Americans today believe criticism to be something that is not just "usually" unfavorable, but *always* unfavorable.

In practice, the *unwitting* use of negative criticism

in daily life is far more common—and far more damaging—than its *deliberate* use. Those we love or live with are seldom aware of the impact of their casual critical words. "Sticks and stones may break my bones, but words will never hurt me," runs the proverb. But if ever a proverb was wide of the mark, that one is. As most people ruefully know, words can do more lasting damage than most physical blows.

"A constant stream of negative remarks—sarcasm, doubts, rebuffs, put-downs—cut emotional scars into even the sturdiest ego," says Dr. Honor Whitney, a family therapist who has spent many years studying the effects of destructive remarks on personality. "Ultimately," she says, "negative statements seriously undermine the way people feel about themselves. The self-image, the inner sense of value as an individual, is weakened."[2]

For example, a slim and attractive woman, fashionably dressed except for her flat-heeled shoes, stated that what she most vividly recalled from her childhood was being teased by her family about her height.

My dad always referred to me as "Skyscraper." He would say things like "How'd you ever get so tall when your mother and I are short?" The words were always said in a jesting tone, but the message I got was that my height was my fault, and that I was being criticized for it. By the time I was fifteen I was convinced I was a gangly freak no boy would ever date. It was years before I developed any confidence with men. I still feel awkward with most of them.

In another instance a successful Los Angeles attorney recalled how, when he was fourteen, he had been invited by a cousin in New York City to spend part of summer vacation there.

I was thrilled because I'd never been that far away from home before. But my mother said I couldn't go off on my own—that I'd get on the wrong plane, or lose my ticket, or get sick. I remember her exact words: "You're just helpless without me to look after you." I knew that wasn't true, but she made me feel so incompetent I figured she was probably right. And you know something? Every time I start on a trip I get butterflies in my stomach. I still think I'm going to do something wrong or stupid.

Why does criticism, in the traditional sense, have these destructive effects?

For one thing, criticism seems to foreclose the possibility of improvement. By focusing almost entirely on *past* action—something someone said or did, or failed to say or do—conventional criticism converts a potentially open-ended situation, one that holds out hope of change for the better, into an immutable negative event. Rarely is anyone told he or she is *doing* something wrong; rather, one is usually told one *did* something wrong. The critic not only "fixes" the incident in the past, but implies that the behavior is unalterable in the future. Thus Eileen used Ken's single lapse of attention on the freeway to label him a permanently incompetent driver.

Second, conventional criticism is almost exclusively a one-way process. The critic speaks and, having spoken, assumes he or she need not say or do anything more. When Sally's boss tossed her sketches back at her, he gave her no opportunity to explain or defend her work. He made no allowance for feedback. Nor did he commit himself to share in the criticism process by making any suggestion as to how she should revise them.

Because the one-way thrust of most criticism is so wholly negative, the person being criticized tends to react negatively as well. First there is the intellectual assumption of guilt, fault or error: *I did something wrong.* Next there follows a surge of anger, resentment, and defensiveness, along with a need for self-justification. Finally, these emotions may be acted out in negative, and certainly nonproductive, behavior—shouting denials, hitting back verbally, crying, or retreating into sullen silence.

The third reason criticism is usually destructive is that it tends to be unfairly selective. Here is an example.

To celebrate her husband's birthday, Joan planned a surprise dinner party for a few of his closest friends. She decorated the dining room, bought two bottles of fine wine, and prepared an elaborate meal, including a new gourmet recipe for the main course and her husband's favorite homemade cheesecake for dessert.

When the last guest had left, Joan asked her husband if he had enjoyed the evening. He considered a moment before replying, then said, "Why do you always experiment with food when we're having company? I didn't think that new recipe turned out well at all."

Though it selected only one element to find fault with, that criticism implicitly put down everything Joan had done to make the evening a success. No matter that she had tried to please her husband; no matter that she had put time, thought and effort into the party; no matter that she had invited his favorite people and baked his favorite dessert; no matter that she may have done a dozen things perfectly and only one with which he could find fault. Her husband's selective criticism left Joan feeling that the entire evening had been a failure.

Let's go back to the concept of criticism. Originally, *criticism* was meant to denote a neutral, objective appraisal of ideas and actions. (The Greek word *kritikos* means "able to discern or judge.") One who criticized was expected to assess the merits as well as the demerits of an object or situation, and to make judgments accordingly. The goals of criticism were to communicate, to influence, to motivate.

Criticism of that sort played an important and positive role in the evaluation process. It helped one look realistically at one's aims and actions; it pointed the way toward new resources and skills; it increased one's tolerance for a variety of opinions. But somehow this concept of criticism became skewed until, finally, only the negative connotations of the word remained.

It is time, we suggest, to redefine criticism in such a way as to change that frame of reference and thus improve both the way we give criticism and the way we take it. Consider this new definition of *criticize:* to communicate information to others in a way that enables them to use it to their advantage and benefit. And *criticism:* a tool to encourage and enhance personal growth and relationships.

This redefining of terms involves more than mere playing with words. The revised definitions can change what psychologists call our "cognitive set"— the way both giver and receiver of criticism are prepared to think about what they say and hear.

The new definition, for example, no longer identifies criticized behavior as an irrevocable act, but as behavior that is capable of change. The new definition makes it clear that criticism is a positive interaction between giver and receiver. With both persons involved, the criticizer is likely to be more sensitive to what he or she is saying, to how it is said, and to the effect the words may have.

The message behind the criticism then becomes, *I am telling you this because I think it can help you and can help our relationship.* By the same token the recipient, instead of feeling hurt or defensive, is more likely to try to integrate the criticism into future actions. Instead of thinking, *He is always carping at me,* the criticized person may think, *He is trying to help me.* In short, both giver and receiver recognize that they are taking part in a growth process.

But do you respond this way?

Think back to the last time you were criticized and how you reacted to what was said.

—What did the words *mean* to you? Did you interpret them as an attack? A put-down? An attempt to help you see what you were doing wrong?

—How did you *feel* when you were being criticized? Angry? Hurt? Rejected? Ashamed? Did your heart start to beat faster? Did you blush? Did your muscles suddenly tense?

—What did you *do*? Did you listen to the criticism silently, or try to interrupt the other person to defend yourself? Did you raise your voice? Walk away? Pound the table? Cry?

Now recall the last time you criticized someone and ask yourself the same three questions: What did I *think* I was saying? How did I *feel* when I said it? How did I *behave* as I was saying it, and after I had finished?

Each of these three factors is individually significant both in giving and receiving criticism. More important, each interacts with and reinforces the other two. How we interpret criticism intellectually affects the way we react to it emotionally. How we react emotionally determines in large measure what we do about it. And because we tend to put subjective labels on our feelings and actions, those two responses in turn influence—often incorrectly—the meaning we attribute to the criticism: *If I feel ashamed, I must have done something bad. . . . If I argue loudly, I must be angry.*

Before you can begin to develop the skills needed to give and receive criticism responsibly and effectively, you must examine more closely how your thoughts, feelings and actions affect your total response to criticism.

How Thought Influences Criticism

"Men are not troubled by things themselves, but by their thoughts about them," observed the philosopher Epictetus two thousand years ago. Psychologists today agree. It is the meaning we assign to events that gives them the power to affect us for good or ill. At least three aspects of "thought" help to influence the way we construe criticism.

Individual Appraisal

Appraisal is a mental process which helps us to define what is happening to or around us. Its roots lie in the special qualities and circumstances—family background, natural talents, physical appearance and health, systems of belief, fears and hopes—that shape our personalities. These combine to form the basis for the unique way each of us interprets our surroundings, gives meaning to outside events, and appraises the situations we encounter in daily life, as the following example demonstrates.

> *Louise, an attractive woman with an abrasive personality, had never been able to maintain a relationship with a man. Men were at first enticed by her looks, but her aggressiveness even-*

tually drove them away. Louise hoped it would be different with Nick, for she had begun to care very much for him.

Nick usually telephoned Louise early on Thursday evenings to make plans for the weekend. When eight o'clock had passed one Thursday evening and Nick hadn't called, Louise called him. She phoned three times in the next two hours, leaving a message each time. When he hadn't returned her calls by midnight, Louise was furious. She took it as a personal affront.

"I knew it was Nick's way of saying he wasn't interested in seeing me anymore," Louise said. "He was telling me to get lost."

Louise's story is significant because it shows that the way we appraise an event dictates not only how we will feel about it, but what action we are likely to take in response to it. Insecure, probably half expecting Nick to abandon her like all the other men she'd known, Louise was distressed not because he had failed to call, but because she had interpreted his silence as implicit criticism, as an indication that he no longer wanted to see her.

The same incident, appraised differently, could have yielded quite a different set of reactions. For instance, what if Louise had chosen to think that Nick had been detained longer than he expected on one of his frequent out-of-town business trips? She might still have been annoyed by his failure to let her know he'd be away, or by his failure to call her long distance, but she would hardly have jumped to the conclusion that he was breaking off their relationship.

Criticism Means Grow! **13**

Instead of interpreting the situation to mean *He doesn't want to see me anymore*, she would more likely have thought, *He's probably too busy to call tonight*. And what if Louise had decided that Nick's failure to phone or to return her calls meant that he might be ill or in an accident? Far from feeling put down or angry, she would have felt concerned and sympathetic.

How we interpret any situation obviously will vary with the circumstances. The point is that however we appraise it, that cognitive choice triggers the feelings and behavior that follow.

When two persons are involved, each may appraise the same situation in contrary ways. In fact, because our perceptions and appraisals are always uniquely individual, it would seem improbable that the appraisals of two separate people could ever completely coincide.

Jeff and Ellen had been engaged for six months when Ellen suddenly ended their relationship. Jeff was astonished. "I had never felt so close to a woman," he said. "There was nothing we couldn't talk about. True, we argued a lot. But the fact that we could argue with each other and still feel close told me we had a really solid basis for marriage."

But Ellen saw things in another light. "We were constantly arguing. I finally realized that we could never get along together."

Both Ellen and Jeff agreed there were many arguments between them, but they appraised that fact differently. Jeff interpreted it as a positive value in their relationship; Ellen saw it as evidence that they were mismatched.

Each person has his or her own perspective. An oversized sofa, for example, will have quite different implications for an upholsterer, a couple in love, and a moving man. Seat four people at a card table and place a block "M" on it. Depending on where each sits, they will see it as an "M," an "E," a "W," or an angular "3."

In the same way, how a person responds to criticism depends to some extent on where he or she mentally "sits." One person may be insulted, another depressed, a third angry, and, far less frequently, still another grateful for having had a flaw pointed out. Or the same individual may respond to the same criticism in all of these different ways at different times, as his or her appraisal of it changes. How often after delivering a critical remark are we surprised at the reaction it produces, especially when we meant our words to be helpful? "You took what I said the wrong way," we protest. Fortunately, as we will see later on, most people can learn to modify the way they appraise criticism so that they are better able to accept it in a positive light.

Level of Expectation

A second "thought process" that influences our response to criticism is governed by *expectations*—the standards we have, the goals we set for ourselves and for those around us, and the mental "bets" we make concerning the outcome of future events. Most people believe it is important to have high expectations. But when the desirable results we anticipate are not forthcoming, criticism of our efforts to achieve them can be much harder to take.

Molly graduated from a prestigious law school in the top five percent of her class. She was offered a job with a major law firm and leaped at the opportunity. She knew it was only a matter of time before her talents would be recognized and rewarded. So when one of the senior partners asked her to draft an important brief for him, Molly worked days, nights, and weekends until she felt she had produced an outstanding report.

"When the partner called me in to his office to go over my draft, I expected nothing but praise," Molly said. "I even had visions of a raise or a promotion. Instead, he said that while I'd made 'a good beginning,' there was a lot more that needed to be done. He pointed out several areas that needed clarification, elaborating on what I'd overlooked until I felt like a first-year student all over again.

"When I left his office I felt crushed . . . a complete failure. When some of my colleagues asked me how it had gone, I was too embarrassed to tell them. I felt I had given the assignment my best shot—and messed up my big chance."

Realistically, there was no reason for Molly to feel put down or ashamed. She *had* done a good job on her first important assignment. Any other young lawyer might have been proud to be told that his or her work was a "good beginning," and even pleased to get specific guidance from a veteran attorney. But Molly had set her expectations so high that even the mildest criticism was devastating. She had become so emotionally involved in her projected goal and the rewards it would bring that when reality fell short of her expectations, it was all the more frustrating.

Molly's reaction was typical: When high expectations for ourselves are not met, any criticism is almost always appraised in a negative light. Logic to the contrary, its message is that we have failed. Because Molly expected so much of herself, she was in effect criticizing *herself*. But criticism can also be ineffective or destructive when we have fixed or unrealistic expectations for the behavior of *others*.

Paul and Leslie had lived together for nearly two years before they got married. Although both had worked during that time, Leslie had made a special effort to keep their two-room apartment attractive and orderly. Shortly after the wedding they moved into a six-room house. Several weeks later many cartons were still unopened, pictures and curtains not hung, and furniture not properly arranged. Paul felt he had a legitimate complaint.

"I don't understand why this place is still such a mess," he said. "Our books and records are still

packed away, I can't find my tools, and you've hardly done a thing about decorating!"

"Listen, half of these cartons are filled with your stuff," Leslie retorted. "I don't know where you want things to go! I can't move furniture by myself! And I go to work just like you do! Why are you blaming me for everything?"

Actually, Paul wasn't *blaming* Leslie for anything. He had merely been *expecting* her to take care of all the household chores as she had in the past. But he was overlooking the fact that their new home was much larger, that Leslie had been promoted to a more demanding job, and that he was not shouldering his share of the marital responsibilities (as Leslie, perhaps, expected he would). As a result, Paul's criticism of Leslie was ineffective and hurtful because, based as it was on unrealistic expectations, it lacked validity. So far as Leslie was concerned, the criticism was totally unjustified.

Expecting someone to continue to act in a way that we have found objectionable in the past is likely to make us more critical more often. It may even lead to *anticipatory criticism*—negative remarks made before the other person does or says anything.

This principle, too, applies both to oneself and to others. Let's assume that an overweight person has failed several times to stick to a diet. As he prepares to start a new diet, he fears he will be tempted once again to sneak forbidden foods. *If I do that,* he says to himself, *I deserve to be fat.* Each time he so much as glances longingly at a doughnut he puts himself down for "weakness." And when, after three weeks of scrupulous dieting, the man indulges in a mildly caloric dessert, he castigates himself for "failing" again. He completely ignores the fact that he has followed his diet more thoroughly than anyone—except himself—might have expected. He is, we say, being too hard on himself. Indeed, he is so critical of his own behavior that he may go off the diet completely and never try to lose weight again.

Expecting someone else to do something we don't like (or *not* to do something we approve of) also tends to increase the intensity and frequency of criticism.

> *"How many times have I told you to make your bed and clean up your room?" Johnny's mother angrily said to him early one Saturday morning.*
>
> *"I'm going to do it as soon as I finish breakfast," Johnny protested.*
>
> *"Well," Mother replied sarcastically, "I'll believe that when I see it. I can't understand how you get your room so messy in the first place!"*
>
> *"Gee," complained Johnny, "you never give me a chance. You start yelling at me for not doing something even when I'm going to do it."*

Here is another example of the effect of negative expectations on criticism.

> *Jane and David traveled a good deal, and whenever it was not feasible to take their seven-year-old, Debbie, with them, Jane's mother would gladly babysit. She adored her grand-*

daughter. But as much as David appreciated his mother-in-law's help, he was irritated by her habit of spoiling the child.

"Every time we come home from a trip Debbie has a dozen new toys, she's gained weight from all the sweets Gram feeds her, and we can't get her to bed at night because Gram has let her stay up late. It's like coming back to a different child."

David had repeatedly asked his mother-in-law not to do these things. "But my criticism had no effect. Gram always said she would stop spoiling Debbie, yet each time the same thing happened," he said.

"Last month, when Gram came to stay with Debbie for the weekend, the first thing she took out of her suitcase was a new toy. I told her right then and there that if she was going to keep on spoiling Debbie, we would hire a babysitter! I figured it was better to have the whole thing out and settled right away than to wait until we got back home. But it started an argument. Gram said she had realized I was right and had brought only the one toy. She said it wasn't fair for me to criticize her for something she wasn't going to do."

Criticizing others prematurely on the basis of what we expect their behavior to be has the effect of "freezing" past events and actions—fixing the past as an inevitable pattern for the future and leaving no room for the possibility of change. Worse, criticism founded on expectations may well turn into a self-fulfilling prophecy. Anyone who knows he will be criticized in advance for something he is expected to do (or not do) may eventually decide there is no point in trying to change his behavior.

Power of Private Speech

A third cognitive process that affects the way we react to criticism is *private speech*—the things we silently "say" when we criticize someone, or when we are (or think we are) about to be criticized.

When you are criticized, do you tend to tell yourself, *Oh-oh, I'm in trouble again,* or *Now I'll have a chance to find out what I did wrong?* When you give criticism, do you tend to silently say, *How dumb can this person be?* or *I'm going to try to be helpful?*

Since, as we have seen, most people assume that criticism is going to be negative, most such "self-statements" also tend to be negative:

The boss wants to talk to me? I hope I don't get fired.
Why do they always pick on me?
This is going to be terrible.
I'm not going to take it anymore!

Or, when one is delivering criticism:
Why can't he/she ever do anything right?
I wish I didn't have to say this.

Private speech is a double-edged implement. On the one hand, it reflects the appraisal we *already* have made of a criticism. On the other hand, private speech influences how we are *likely* to appraise criticism, because it tends to confirm and objectify our abstract expectations.

Private speech also contributes to the way we feel and act in response to criticism. Hostile or denigrating self-statements provoke negative physical and emotional reactions. For example, if a youngster is told to report to the principal's office and says to himself, *What did I do wrong this time?* he will probably begin to feel anxious, angry or guilty. He may enter the office wearing a hangdog look or nervously clenching his fists. But if he says to himself, *Maybe I've been voted into the honor society,* he will feel hopeful, walk with a springy step, and have a smile ready.

Private speech sets into motion a closed circuit that can work in two directions. As we shall see, you can learn to control private speech so that it leads to positive rather than negative attitudes.

How Feelings Affect Criticism

We tend to think of an emotion as a disembodied sentiment. We say we feel sad or glad, calm or angry, romantic or depressed. But an emotion is more than that; it is the product of physiological changes to which we attach a subjective mental label. In other words, what we think has a good deal to do with how we identify and label whatever kind of bodily arousal we are experiencing.

For example, as Lynn dresses for an evening date with the man she loves, she can sense her heart beating a bit faster. Because she anticipates a pleasurable experience, she says she feels "excited" or "happy." As she walks down a dark street on the way to her car, Lynn hears ominous footsteps behind her. Again her heart beats faster. Now, however, she feels "frightened." The same change in the level of physical arousal—the increased heartbeat—has been relabeled a totally different emotion.

Because criticism is traditionally thought of as negative or destructive, the bodily arousal (or "feeling") that occurs when we are criticized—muscle tension, faster heartbeat, a surge of blood pressure—is usually given an unpleasant label: anger, frustration, anxiety, resentment.

Sarah, a 23-year-old student-teacher, found it increasingly difficult to tolerate the criticism she received from her supervisor whenever he observed her teaching a class.

I didn't know how much longer I could take it. My supervisor harped on everything I did. I was anxious enough about teaching the class, but by the time he was through criticizing me, I was a wreck.

When he asked to speak to me, I always experienced the same feeling—a sinking in the pit of my stomach. I dreaded hearing what he had to say. I told myself, "Well, here it comes again," and I was always right. When I left his office I felt like throwing things—and I often did!

Sarah's case illustrates the interaction among thoughts, feelings and behavior.

—Because Sarah consistently appraised her supervisor's criticism of her teaching as a negative encounter, she developed a negative attitude toward it.

—This negative attitude influenced the emotional label Sarah placed on her physical reactions to his criticism.

—Since the entire sequence—negative attitude, level of arousal and label ("sinking" feeling)—repeated itself each time, the criticism became an increasingly destructive experience for her. In effect, Sarah told herself that when the supervisor called her to his office, she was going to have a particular set of emotional responses. Sarah anticipated these responses because she expected to feel anxious and upset. Sarah's self-statement—*Here it comes again*—influenced the way she would feel by telling her what kind of arousal she should experience, and by providing a label for it.

How Criticism Affects Behavior

The third factor which influences our attitude toward criticism is overt behavior—how we act when we are criticized. When Sarah walked out of her supervisor's office and threw something, she was behaviorally confirming her cognitive and emotional responses. Since we often allow our behavior to dictate the way we interpret our feelings *(If I'm yelling, I must be angry ... If I am running away, I must be afraid)*, Sarah's actions helped to perpetuate the destructive cycle.

To a large degree, behavior is a product of learning. When we consistently register the same basic response to the same basic stimulus, an association is formed between the two. If the results are assessed as favorable, most likely we will continue to use the behavior that brought them about. If the results are viewed as unfavorable, the behavior tends not to be repeated. It is important to remember that it is not the result itself that counts, but the way we interpret it. What seems an inappropriate or negative outcome to one person may be interpreted as an appropriate or proper outcome to another person.

Consider, for example, the case of Robert E., a 35-year-old staff assistant to a state legislator. "When the Senator criticizes something I've done," Robert says, "I am able to sit down and listen calmly until he has had his say. Since we have worked together for many years, I'm able to tell him frankly what I think and how I feel about his comments. Most of the time we keep a dialogue going until the problem is straightened out. I seldom get upset by his criticisms, and the Senator respects me for that."

But the scenario is quite different when Robert is criticized by his wife: "I can't stand it," he says bluntly. "I get angry, I interrupt, I reject her criticism and start to point out *her* flaws. Then she yells at me and starts to cry. Usually the battle ends when I tell her to shut up, and she walks out of the room. It's often an hour or more before we can behave toward each other like human beings again."

Why does Robert react so differently toward criticism from his boss and from his wife? He has learned that the way he responds to his boss has had—and will probably continue to have—what Robert considers to be a favorable outcome. He gets a chance to state his own position and he gains his employer's respect.

But, you may say, surely the repeated and unresolved conflict that criticism sparks between Robert and his wife is not a favorable outcome. Why then does he continue to respond so angrily to her? The answer is that while the result might not be considered productive by most people, it works for Robert. He learned early in his marriage that yelling produced a positive result for him: the criticism ceased, an unpleasant confrontation was cut short, and, after a short period of tension, life returned to normal.

In short, though Robert's behavioral response to criticism is in one instance destructive and in the other constructive, he has learned that both in their own ways produce favorable results for him. (The results, incidentally, are also favorable for Robert's boss and wife. The Senator is pleased that he has an intelligent assistant who is willing to listen and learn. The wife is relieved because, when she walks out of the room, she is rid of the necessity to continue arguing and perhaps risk making matters worse.) In each case the way Robert acts strongly influences the way he thinks and feels about criticism. The lesson is clear: If we can bring some control to bear on our behavior, we can to some degree control—and perhaps change—our thoughts and feelings.

2 | "I Don't Know How to Tell You This, But..."

Criticism plays a key role in social intercourse. It can be used to motivate people, to influence them, to teach them, to communicate needs and desires, or to encourage self-improvement. Yet what we say and how we say it are all too often at odds with what we hope to accomplish.

> WIFE: Must you always wear such sloppy old clothes around the house? You look like a bum!
>
> HUSBAND: What do you want me to do, wear a tuxedo?

> ————

> SUPERVISOR: This is the third time in a month you've been late with the production report. All I hear from you is excuses. I'm warning you, you'd better shape up, or else!

EMPLOYEE (mumbling to himself): So fire me . . . I'm sick of your threats.

———

HUSBAND: We'll miss the train if you don't stop fussing with your makeup. We're always late because of you.
WIFE: It's not my fault! You make me nervous when I'm getting ready to go out.

If the ultimate goal of criticism is to promote change for the better, none of the examples quoted above has much chance of achieving that end. Each of the complaints may be well founded; that is, at least they identify behavior which can be realistically irritating. But the manner and tone in which each critic conveys annoyance or dissatisfaction are almost guaranteed to make matters worse—to thwart rather than foster a constructive response.

Unfortunately, most people seem to believe that for a criticism to be effective it must be delivered in a biting, unfeeling way, even though this may go against the better nature of the criticizer. The evidence is the semiapologetic, often self-serving remarks with which we so often preface our critical comments: "I hate to say this, but . . ." or "I know you won't believe me, but I'm telling you this for your own good."

If we don't actually say these things, we think them. And implicit in each such statement is the assumption that however useful a particular criticism is *meant* to be, it is bound to deflate an ego, wound someone's feelings or denigrate someone's ability.

Therein lies the paradox of criticism. On the one hand, we think it will help the recipient; on the other we fear it will hurt his or her feelings. Most of the time criticism does fall into the second category. Most of the time it focuses on finding faults, exposing weaknesses, downgrading ideas, belittling efforts. Indeed, delivering critical put-downs may be one of the great national pastimes.

But if criticism can help us, why should we fear it? One answer is that we are so accustomed to thinking of critical remarks as destructive that we overlook their constructive value. Another is that we seldom know how to offer criticism in a positive way.

To gather data for her doctoral dissertation, "Criticism and Interaction," sociologist Stephanie Hughes designed an experiment to test the way people use and respond to criticism. She asked a group of women volunteers to invent a new kind of game that could be played with dominoes. Another group of volunteers was told to respond to half of the suggestions with positive criticism (focusing on both the merits and demerits of a suggestion, but emphasizing the former), and to half with negative criticism (focusing only on the demerits of a suggestion). In subsequent debriefing sessions Hughes analyzed the attitudes and feelings aroused in both sets of volunteers by the two different types of criticism.

When the criticizers knew they were to use a negative approach, that expectation colored their attitude. Some said they felt hostile or competitive toward the person suggesting the game. For instance, Hughes reported, one critic said she found herself "trying to pick up on something about the other per-

son that bothers me, so I can give negative criticism."
Another said that "giving negative criticism puts me
in a negative state of mind, so I can't think highly of
anything" that is suggested. Expecting to give negative criticism, said Hughes, evidently actually creates
a negative mind-set.

The volunteers who received negative criticism for
their suggestions of new games were shaken by it.
They tended to interpret even mildly negative comments to mean that their ideas were "bad" ideas.
Moreover, they were influenced to a considerable
degree by even the slightest downgrading of their
suggestions. Many who at first felt their ideas for
new games were reasonably good decided, after
negative criticism, that the ideas were not only "less
good" but were more or less "bad."[3]

Clearly, the person criticizing and the person
being criticized both contribute to, and are the vic-
tims of, the counterproductive effects of destructive
criticism. If this were a deliberate pattern of behavior it might almost be easier to deal with. But the dis-
mal fact is that most people express criticism
negatively without seeming to realize the impact of
their words, or the barriers that block the path to
constructive criticism.

Destructive Criticism

Let's look first at the factors responsible for destructive patterns of giving criticism. Later in this chapter
we will examine the factors involved in destructive
responses to criticism.

Shaming the Receiver

Certain forms of criticism almost guarantee that no constructive purpose will be served; embarrassing, shaming, or humiliating the receiver falls into this category.

> *We were dressing to go to dinner with friends and, as we usually do, my wife and I asked each other how we looked. "Are you really going to wear that shirt?" my wife asked tartly. "Why? It looks all right to me," I said. "The collar is too short," she said. "It's completely out of style." I told her I didn't care much about style, and she said, "I know—that's why you always look tacky. Sometimes I'm embarrassed to be seen with you."*
>
> *That remark really got to me, it was so uncalled-for. Next thing I knew I was criticizing her outfit. "Your dress is much too tight. It makes you look five pounds fatter." Both of us ended up trying to outridicule the other's appearance, saying things we didn't mean. But they hurt just the same. The evening was ruined.*

Apart from its crudeness, shaming another person is a counterproductive way to criticize. Almost invariably it provokes rejection of the criticism—*I don't look tacky . . . I am not fat*—as well as defensive retaliation. Both perpetuate the destructive cycle.

Helpful criticism tries to make a distinction between the behavior being criticized and the individual involved. Shaming deliberately links the two. It moves from specific detail to generalizations about overall behavior. "Your shirt is out of style" (specific) becomes "You always look tacky"; "Your dress is too tight" (specific) becomes "You're getting fat."

A "shaming" criticism can also be conveyed indirectly. One way is to make an invidious comparison: "My father wouldn't wear a shirt like that." Another is to use sarcasm: "Are you going to be able to breathe in that dress?"

Sometimes criticizing by shaming does not require words at all. A Swedish husband once gave his wife, as an anniversary present, a necklace made of three hundred buttons she had neglected to sew on his shirts and jackets! (But she had the last laugh; she used the necklace as evidence of mental cruelty in her successful suit for divorce.)

The addition of a "shaming" element can make an otherwise tolerable criticism totally unacceptable. It represents an explicit attack on one's self-esteem.

Assigning Blame

Criticism is destructive when we use words and phrases that indicate we think the behavior at issue was done on purpose.

> BOSS TO SECRETARY: This letter is riddled with typographical errors! You don't seem to care what kind of work you turn out.

> ———

> PARENT TO CHILD: Look at your clothes! Why do you always have to get yourself so filthy?

Blaming assumes that we know the intent of the person we are criticizing. Possible alternative explanations—such as a person's level of experience or ability, accidental mistakes, time pressure—are not taken into consideration. As a result blamers often find themselves "lecturing" the other person, dealing in accusations, loaded questions, and generalizations such as "always" and "never."

The response to blaming, like the response to shaming, is defensive. The criticized person feels he or she must prove the charge is false. But when one person is busy accusing and the other busy defending, the substance of the criticism itself is seldom dealt with constructively.

Faulty Feedback

When critical remarks fail to be specific, they limit the possibility that the person being criticized will receive and act upon them in a manner satisfactory to the critic. Ian, a staff writer on a magazine, attests to this in recalling his early days on the job.

They were the most frustrating of my life, not because I kept getting my copy tossed back at me for rewrites and revisions, but because I never was told clearly what was wrong with it. My editor would mark up a paragraph or a page with marginal comments like "Fix this!" or "Needs more oomph!" Sometimes there would just be a row of question marks. I was completely depressed because I couldn't tell what he felt was wrong, or exactly what he wanted me to do.

Ian's experience reflects the ineffective result of faulty critical feedback. It occurs when the criticizer fails to explain precisely what is being (or has been) done badly or what steps can be taken to correct or improve matters. Because such criticism is characterized by vagueness, the response tends to be a feeling of confusion and helplessness. One tends to think that whatever one does, the result will be the same— so why try to do anything about it. Instead of shedding light on a problem or clarifying an issue, faulty feedback usually leads to unintentional repetition of the criticized behavior.

Unstated Assumptions

Unstated assumptions are closely related to faulty feedback in that the criticizer takes it for granted that the other person understands the criticism. For example, a college senior working on a thesis for a psychology degree consulted frequently with his advisor. "There were times when the professor pointed out where I'd gone wrong in handling my statistics," the student said. "But though I knew what she was saying, I didn't really *understand* what I was supposed to do to correct my procedures. The professor just assumed I knew what she meant. And I was too embarrassed to admit that I didn't."

The unstated assumption not only makes accurate communication more difficult, it also makes the criticized person feel depersonalized. As we pointed out earlier, criticism should lead to an exchange of information between giver and receiver. In this case, the criticizer was merely handing out information without asking for a response.

Unclear Alternatives

Once a criticism has been made, the person criticized may find it useful to ask the criticizer to recommend an alternative course of action. It is the responsibility of the criticizer to be prepared to offer one.

Carolyn, a 25-year-old secretary to the marketing manager of an electronics firm, worked for a man who held her accountable for managing his affairs, but did nothing to help her manage them.

> *"I didn't mind being criticized by my boss. I expect some of that on a job. What bothered me was that he never gave me a clue to how I could work things out more efficiently and avoid slip-ups."*
>
> *Because Carolyn's boss was out of his office much of the day, messages and memos piled up. Carolyn would stack the memos and the slips of paper with the names and telephone numbers of people he was supposed to call on top of the "in" box on his desk. "But he didn't always check the box carefully," Carolyn said, "and when he missed important messages or meetings, he blamed me.*
>
> *"After a while I left the memos right on his desk, and if I saw him in the hallway I would remind him to look for them when he got back*

*to his office. Of course that didn't work too well,
because I didn't always see him. And sometimes,
to be honest, I would forget to remind him. So I
still got blamed if he missed an appointment.*

*"I even tried keeping my own list of things to
tell him about, but most of the time he'd say, 'Not
now, Carolyn, I'm too busy. Tell me later.' Of
course 'later' was usually too late. After that I
just didn't know how to handle things, and I got
so concerned about getting messages to my boss
that I began to foul up some of my other work."*

Most of us can empathize with Carolyn because
most of us have been criticized in the same manner—blamed for a muddled situation without being
given any suggestions or alternatives that might improve it. Carolyn's boss criticized her for missed messages, but he never tried to help her deal with the
problem. He might have suggested putting a message
board on the wall over his desk, where he couldn't
help seeing it. He might have checked with her by
phone every hour to pick up his messages verbally.
The point is that the boss did not follow through on
his criticism with procedural alternatives. He left
Carolyn with a sense of failure.

Emotional Detractors

Criticism that is not separated from the critic's personal feelings of irritation or disappointment is
bound to have a destructive effect. Granted, it is hard
to detach one's emotions from the content of one's
words, or to speak dispassionately when one feels

strongly. But shouting in anger, laughing in ridicule, frowning or grimacing in disapproval—all *detract* from what one is trying to convey. The boss who yells at a hapless employee, or the teacher who makes fun of a youngster who can't answer a question, not only abuses criticism but negates it. Their words will have no useful influence on the criticized person's behavior because the latter is more likely to react to the unpleasant emotional overtones of the criticism than to its substance. Anger will be met by fear (or anger), and ridicule by resentment. Whatever good the intent of the criticism might have accomplished is lost in the welter of clashing emotions.

It is virtually impossible to understand and evaluate criticism when either giver or receiver is under emotional stress. As a result, little or no behavior change is likely to occur. This, in turn, will justify, or at least reinforce, the criticizer's negative attitude: *He didn't pay any attention to what I said and still makes the same mistakes. Now I'm really angry!* The criticizer's counterproductive emotions interact with the criticized person's negative responses to perpetuate a destructive circle. (See "Interfering Emotions" on page 52 for a discussion of how even positive criticism can be heard in a destructive way.)

Emphasizing the Negative

Both Nancy and Glen enjoyed Chinese food. When Nancy learned that a class in Chinese cuisine was being offered at the local college, she immediately enrolled. Glen was delighted. He looked forward to mouth-watering Chinese meals at home. But Nancy explains what happened.

The class was eight weeks long. When it was over I felt I'd learned a great deal. To try out my new skills I prepared an elaborate six-course dinner. Perhaps I should have started out with something simpler, but I really wanted to show Glen everything I'd learned. I even bought a pair of Chinese pajamas to wear while serving the meal.

But do you think Glen appreciated my efforts? He had some unpleasant comment to make about every dish. The hot-and-sour soup was not spicy enough. The sweet-and-sour fish was too sour. The egg rolls were not crisp enough to suit him. The spareribs were tough and the shrimp dish—my pièce de résistance—he pronounced too greasy. I guess I was lucky that he didn't have any fault to find with the Chinese tea. The final blow was when he said, "No fortune cookies?" I knew it was supposed to be a joke, but I couldn't laugh.

Glen knew how much effort I'd put into the dinner—he knew it was my first try at making all those dishes myself—and yet he couldn't manage to say one complimentary word. All he did was tell me why everything was wrong. Well, I'm through trying. The next time Glen wants to have Chinese food at home he can buy it at a take-out restaurant!

Nancy's is a classic story of emphasizing negatives. Glen not only criticized her for the poor results of

I Don't Know How to Tell You This   **39**

her effort, but pounded home the message that even her effort was not appreciated. In such cases, the recipient's usual reaction is to cease the criticized behavior altogether. And why not? Nancy had no motivation to try to improve her cooking because her first attempt was not reinforced in any positive way. She felt, as most of us would, *Why bother if all I'm going to be told is how terrible everything is?*

Rigid Attitudes

Criticism is frequently prefaced with the words, "You should" or "You shouldn't." Those and similar phrases impede the criticism process for two reasons. First, such attitudes reveal a rigidity in the criticizer. "Should" and "shouldn't" imply that the criticizer's opinion or method is the only "right" one. This in itself is enough to put a damper on anyone's willingness to try to change.

Second, this one-way assumption that the critic's way is the only correct way perpetuates the traditional concept of criticism as an either/or process—that something or someone is "right" or "wrong," and that there is no acceptable middle ground, no acceptable alternative behavior. The criticized person is likely to react defensively: *Why shouldn't I do it my way?* The pattern that results is one of stubborn mutual disagreement.

Environmental Factors

There is a time and a place for every enterprise, and criticism is no exception. Critical remarks which otherwise might be offered and accepted in a positive way can be rendered ineffective not because of what we say, but because of when and where we say it.

Every night when I come home from work my wife is on my back. She doesn't bother to ask how my day went, or to notice if I'm especially tired or depressed. She goes right to it.

Last night the first thing she said to me was that I had forgotten to mail a letter for her, and she had had to make a special trip to the post office. The night before she was at me the minute I walked in because I hadn't left a signed blank check for her to pay the plumber with.

She says I always get angry when she criticizes me. Of course I get angry. I don't mind being criticized—I admit I sometimes forget to do things I promised her I'd do. But I can't stand it when she calls me to account as soon as I walk in the door. I'd like a little time to relax before I hear about what I've done wrong.

=====

I don't think I have ever felt as ashamed or embarrassed as when I was nine years old and in the third grade. There were about twenty-five kids in the class, and one day the teacher told us all to draw a map of the United States. I was pretty good at drawing, and I spent a lot of time making my map as artistic as I could. But I wasn't very good at geography, and I had a lot of states in the wrong places.

When the teacher looked at my work she

started to laugh, and then in a loud voice asked me where I'd gotten the information that South Dakota was right next to South Carolina. The whole class broke into a roar of laughter, and I just wanted to sink through the floor. I didn't even hear what the teacher was saying when she corrected my map.

It is important to be alert to the time, the place, the presence of other people, and the emotional state of the criticized person if you want your criticism to be effective. Anyone who has other things on his mind, or is concerned with what those around him may think, or is depressed, angry or anxious, is not paying attention to what the critic is saying. And certainly criticism under those circumstances is not likely to be helpful. Helen's story is a case in point.

I dented the rear fender of our new car when I was backing out of a supermarket parking lot recently. The damage was minor, both to my car and to the one I collided with, but the shock of the accident left me edgy. As soon as I got home I told my husband what had happened, expecting some sympathy. But instead of asking if I was all right, he glared at me and said, "Do you know how much our insurance is going to cost now? Couldn't you have looked where you were going?" At that instant I couldn't have cared if I had totaled the damn car!

Common sense and a modicum of concern for personal feelings should be sufficient to alert us to the conditions under which we criticize. But when our own emotions are beyond control, or when we think it is essential to deal with the criticized behavior immediately, we ignore the importance of these environmental factors. All too often the inappropriate setting deprives the criticism of its validity.

Threats and Ultimatums

Threatening remarks are certain to detract from the goal of criticism, as the case of Susan, a seventeen-year-old student, illustrates.

> *Every time my father criticizes me, I feel as though I'm being unfairly punished. If I don't "shape up," as he puts it, he threatens to take away my driving privileges, or cut my allowance, or make me stay home on weekends. I never get around to discussing what he objects to, or finding out why he objects to it, because I'm too angry. I simply give in because I'm afraid of what may happen if I don't.*

In another instance a woman dissatisfied with her husband's lovemaking technique bluntly pointed out his failings but made no attempt to tell him what she would prefer him to do. Instead, she undermined his sexual confidence further by saying, "If you don't learn how to please me, I guess I'll have to find someone who can." (Even if the woman had used a subtler version of threat—for instance, becoming increasingly unresponsive to her husband's sexual advances—the result would have been the same.)

The "or else" style of criticism relies on threat to

produce change. But threat either paralyzes the criticized person or produces change for the wrong reasons. Since a threat places "conditions" on a relationship, the criticized person reacts out of anger at or fear of the possible consequences. Behavior *may* be altered, but not because the person agrees with or understands the criticism. This is a good example of how criticism can sometimes be partially effective even while it is destructive. Hitting someone on the head can be an effective way to get his or her attention, but it is not necessarily a constructive way to do so.

In the long run, the continued use of threats as a critical technique becomes totally counterproductive. For one thing, when threats are repeated too often without being carried out, they lose their effectiveness. For another, the criticized person may well call the bluff and challenge the threat: "Or else *what?* So go ahead and do it! I don't care!" Even when such confrontations are resolved, both persons are likely to carry a residue of resentment over into their relationship. We may feel we are always "giving in" or letting the other have his or her way. Threats turn the process of criticism into a power struggle—precisely what it should not become.

"I Told You So"

Strictly speaking, the "I told you so" manner of criticizing is less a way of trying to effect a change in the other person's ideas or behavior than it is of establishing the correctness of one's own. A marital therapist tells of the young couple who were planning their first dinner party for important guests. Sandra had wanted it to be perfect, not so much to impress the guests as to make her husband proud of her. She had made sure their house was spotless, the silver polished, and the china and crystal gleaming. No gourmet cook, Sandra had planned a simple meal. But she had decided to end it with her specialty, a chocolate cream cake she made superbly.

When Sandra told Howard what she was going to serve for dessert, he tried to dissuade her. "It takes a lot of time, and you're going to be rushed anyway. If something goes wrong we won't have any dessert." When Sandra insisted, Howard shrugged and said, "I still think it's a mistake. Keep everything simple. Buy a cake."

The dinner preparations took longer than Sandra expected. She was late getting the cake out of the oven to cool. She waited as long as possible, but, even so, when she unmolded the cake the layers crumbled into fragments on the kitchen counter. Sandra wailed.

At that moment Howard could have offered comforting words. He could have been empathetic: "It's a shame, after you worked so hard." He could have made a helpful suggestion: "We'll cut what's left of the cake into sections and I'll run out and get some ice cream to put over them." Or he could have held Sandra close until she calmed down.

But Howard did none of these things. Instead, he took advantage of the disaster to criticize Sandra, to prove that he had been right all along. "Didn't I tell you it was dumb to try to make that cake?" he said. "Now what are you going to do for dessert?" Sandra knew she'd been wrong. What she needed least at that moment was for Howard to rub her nose in her misjudgment.

The Accusing Question

Criticism by question may seem to be a constructive way of opening a discussion; frequently, however, it puts the criticized person on the defensive. "Is that what you plan to do? What do you think that will accomplish?" "Can't you do that better?" "What makes you think that's a good idea?"

The humanistic therapist Fritz Perls once observed that if you turn a question mark on its side it becomes a "hook." Asking questions that contain implicit criticism is a way of "hooking" the other person into a defensive attitude. For example, a teacher criticizes a student's poorly organized term paper this way:

> TEACHER: Why did you put the section on economics toward the end of your report?
> (STUDENT offers a weak reason.)
> TEACHER: But didn't you realize that . . .

Observe how the first critical question leads to the increasingly destructive second question. But, as we shall see later, questions can also be a technique of constructive criticism. Suppose the teacher had said, "Do you think the section on economics might fit better if you placed it in the first part of your report?" In that case the student would not have been hooked into a defensive or antagonistic stance. He would more likely have felt he was having a useful and helpful discussion.

Destructive Responses

It is not always the criticizer who is responsible when criticism proves fruitless, because criticism can be *taken*, as well as given, in destructive ways. There are four possible "criticism interactions":

$$\text{Constructive Giving} <\begin{array}{l}\text{Destructive Taking} \\ \text{Constructive Taking}\end{array}$$

$$\text{Destructive Giving} <\begin{array}{l}\text{Constructive Taking} \\ \text{Destructive Taking}\end{array}$$

Hurtful criticism can sometimes be salvaged if the recipient accepts it with a positive point of view. But even criticism that is offered constructively is rendered ineffective by a recipient who reacts in a negative way.

Just as there are external and internal factors that hinder the intelligent giving of criticism, so are there barriers—counterproductive thoughts, feelings and behavior—to productive acceptance. An actor's wife, for instance, says her husband is "not good" at taking criticism of his performances. "He can be destroyed by the mildest comment because he magnifies it tenfold." A rock star declares that she reacts to criticism with defiance. "If they call me arrogant, next time I'll be even more arrogant!" Celebrities and public performers are perhaps entitled to be more sensitive to criticism since it can affect their incomes and reputations. But while the response of a public figure may be more vehement, it is not unique. Most people tend to react negatively to criticism at first. Let's look at some of the stratagems and techniques they use.

Stonewalling

In Stephanie Hughes's experiment, you will recall, one volunteer was to suggest ideas for new games that could be played with dominoes while another was to criticize those suggestions, sometimes in a flatly rejecting way, sometimes in a mildly encouraging way. One of the most frequent responses to negative criticism (and occasionally also to positive criticism) was what the researcher called "reiteration."

According to Hughes, much of the time the subject would merely repeat her original suggestion in only slightly different words. Sometimes she would preface the repetition by blaming the criticizer: "You weren't listening," or "What I said was . . ." or "You missed my point." Less frequently the subject would assume the responsibility herself for the need to repeat with a phrase such as, "Perhaps I didn't explain it very well." In either case, Hughes concluded, the idea suggester "used reiteration, more or less openly or deviously, to protect and defend the ideas that had been criticized."[4]

Reiteration is one form of "stonewalling" against

criticism. Instead of opening our minds to whatever may be useful in the criticizer's comments, we block them out in an effort to defend our own ideas. There are many ways to stonewall. We can call on our own experience: "I've been doing it this way for years." We can be rigid or self-righteous: "I hear what you say, but my way (or idea, or opinion) is better than yours." Or we can adopt a fatalistic ("I can't help it") or even anarchic ("I don't care what you say") attitude.

Stonewalling is a destructive response to criticism because it prevents us from exploring alternatives. Ultimately it prevents us from seeing the need to change our ideas or behaviors. By shutting off discussion and setting up a closed communication pattern we block out the chance to gain potentially useful new information or insight.

Excuse Making

"When my son was little he had an excuse for everything," a man recalls. "If his mother or I pointed out that he hadn't put his toys away, or finished his lunch, or done his schoolwork, he would always say, in the same breath, 'Yeah, but . . .' and dredge up an explanation. It got so that for years we called him 'Yebbut.' "

Children are notorious "yebbuts," but so are some adults. Like children, they find it difficult to admit that they are not perfect; difficult to accept responsibility for their actions; difficult to admit the validity of criticism. The "yes" partially acknowledges a flaw in one's behavior; the "but" is a hasty effort to excuse or justify it—and thus to alleviate the stress caused by this crack in one's self-image.

"Yes, but . . ." is a destructive response to criticism because it is a barrier to constructive change. The paradox of change is that you cannot change until you accept who and what you are. Yet dealing with criticism in a "yes, but . . ." manner prevents you from accepting who you are, and thus from acknowledging that there are areas you might want or need to change. If "stonewalling" is a defense of one's ideas, "yes, but . . ." is a defense of one's self-image.

It is destructive, moreover, because it conveys a contradictory message. The use of "but" negates, or at least qualifies, the admission that preceded it. "Yes, I was wrong, but I was told to do it that way" actually implies "No, I *wasn't* wrong *because* I was told to do it that way." Or, "Yes, I made a mistake, but I had too many other things on my mind" implies "No, I *didn't* make a mistake *because* I had too many other things on my mind to be expected not to foul up one of them." In an attempt to "protect" himself against criticism that he hears as an attack on his self-image, the "yebbut" is thinking of his defense even before the criticizer is finished speaking.

The Retaliatory Exchange

> SYLVIA: I asked you to mail this letter to my mother two days ago, and here it is still on the hall table. Don't you ever remember anything? You have a mind like a sieve.

HERBERT: You're a fine one to talk. Who forgot to take my good suit to the cleaners? Anyway, you always write to your mother. Couldn't you take the time to drop a line to my folks once in a while? You know how busy I am.

SYLVIA (sarcastically): I certainly do. You're always busy, especially when I want you to do something with me. But you have time to play golf with your cronies.

HERBERT: That's relaxation. When I'm with you, you always find something to nag me about. You've gotten to be an awful nag, Sylvia.

And so on, interminably, the "topper" pattern continues with each responding to the criticism he or she receives by criticizing the criticizer. Retaliatory criticism perpetuates a destructive interaction by blurring the focus of the original statement. Does this man in fact usually forget to do what his wife asks? If so, is there some way he can correct this shortcoming? This couple will never find out because the issue is quickly buried under a succession of unrelated criticisms. Instead of dealing with the criticized behavior the couple engages in a mutual put-down session.

Avoidance and Withdrawal

Withdrawal/avoidance is another destructive response style. The teenager criticized for not helping around the house, or for playing the stereo too loud, retreats to his or her room and slams the door. The employee criticized for doing a poor job avoids contact with his boss for the rest of the week. The student criticized by a teacher takes an inconspicuous seat in the classroom. The husband or wife criticized by a partner leaves the room to avoid continuing the discussion.

When we deal with criticism (or more accurately, fail to deal with it) by isolating ourselves from the criticizer, we cut ourselves off from discovering any value the criticism might have. Walking away tends to reinforce our cognitive appraisal of the situation as "unpleasant" and further reinforces the idea of withdrawal as a "solution." If a similar situation arises (or threatens to arise) in the future, it becomes even more likely that we will withdraw from it as well. Avoidance and withdrawal thus tend to become ingrained reactions to criticism. This not only deprives us of any chance to benefit from the criticism, but in the eyes of others marks us as someone who cannot take the heat of criticism.

Superficial Acceptance

Placid agreement with a criticism is a singularly effective way of undermining its value. How often have you heard someone say, "I guess you're right," or "I'm sorry about that"? But verbal acceptance of the criticism is about as far as that person's response goes. By superficially agreeing, he or she is off the hook—free *not* to have to deal with the criticism in a realistic and productive way, and at the same time free to continue the actions that provoked the criticism in the first place. If love means never having to say you're sorry, then saying you're sorry means never having to do anything to change what you are sorry about.

This response to criticism frustrates the criticizer, who is always *hearing* that some change is going to take place but never sees that change actually occur. The criticizer may well feel angry, helpless, and, worse yet, ignored. "My husband never really listened to anything I told him," a woman says. "I was careful to offer criticism only when I felt it was for his own good, and he almost always agreed with what I said. But he seldom made an effort to act on it. I finally decided that he didn't care enough about me to pay attention to my words. Ultimately I couldn't believe *anything* he said because I realized that he used words the way some people use pats on the head—just to pacify me."

Placid agreement is not the same as withdrawal/avoidance. Though both responses make it possible to sidestep criticism, the latter involves physical distancing, which sets up an immediate negative relationship. Agreement implicitly promises that some positive response will occur, and it often takes quite a while before the criticizer discovers that this is an illusion.

Interfering Emotions

You will recall how emotional detractors can have a damaging effect when criticism is given. In the same way, no one can be adequately *receptive* to criticism if he or she is tense, angry or anxious. Negative feelings interfere with a rational appraisal of criticism and undercut whatever constructive use it may have.

"Losing your cool" may well stop others from offering criticism, but that is not necessarily a desirable goal. For example, a retail store salesclerk was frequently reprimanded by her department head for being away from her post while customers were waiting. Whenever this happened she broke into tears. At first the supervisor was taken aback and sought to reassure her. But when the clerk continued to wander away from her post during working hours the crying act merely irritated the supervisor. "We could never talk about what she was doing," the man said, "because her feelings always got in the way. So I had to fire her."

It is important to note that each of the foregoing destructive styles of reacting to criticism has a built-in "reward." The reward is this: the criticized person does not actually have to confront or deal with the criticism in a realistic way—at least for the time being. Self-image is protected; behavior change is avoided. And since all of this can be seen as a small "victory," the negative response is reinforced.

What are the overall results generated by destructive patterns of giving and taking criticism? For one thing, the tension, irritation and psychological distance they create between the criticizer and the person criticized makes future criticism even more difficult and unprofitable. For another, the destructive patterns fail to have any significant positive impact on the behavior at issue. The criticism may indeed continue, but no resolution of the problem is likely.

To change this bleak picture we need to develop two sets of skills. One is to learn how to break the destructive patterns, and techniques for doing so will be discussed in the chapters on criticism's special problem areas—sex, work, and children. The second is to develop constructive techniques for giving and taking criticism. These will be explored in the following two chapters.

3 | How to Give Criticism and Get Results

A man recently decided to stop carping about his wife's poor housekeeping habits. Since his criticisms led only to arguments, he tried a different approach. Saying nothing to his wife, he secreted dollar bills in all of the places he felt she was neglecting.

A day or so later she opened their home freezer and found one of the bills with a note attached to it. The note read: "Reward number one, for defrosting the freezer." Her curiosity piqued, the woman recalled some of the other criticisms her husband had voiced. In a corner of the den she went through a pile of magazines she had long been meaning to clip, save or discard. At the bottom of the pile she found another dollar and another note: "Reward number four, for sorting magazines."

Realizing that rewards number two and three must exist, and that there might be others after number four, she went on a cleaning spree. By the time her treasure hunt ended she had dealt with all the things her husband had been fruitlessly complaining about. And, instead of feeling resentful, she found herself intrigued by the sugar-coated gambit.

This is, admittedly, an unusual case. But it does exemplify the trouble many people have in criticizing others, and the lengths to which they will go to avoid doing so directly. "I always thought it was difficult for me to *take* criticism," one woman says, "but I realize it's much harder for me to *give* it because I don't know how."

To give constructive criticism—and to feel comfortable about it—one must first answer a key question: *How can I convey the information I want to impart so the other person accepts it in a way that will benefit that person, and/or improve our relationship?*

This question shifts the entire frame of reference of criticism from fault finding to problem solving and emphasizes three essential qualities of constructive, or positive, criticism:

1.   It forces the critic to take a harder look at his or her motives for voicing criticism.

2.   It focuses on the possibilities for change and improved behavior.

3.   It acknowledges a commitment between the person giving and the person receiving the criticism—a recognition that both share responsibility for resolving the behavior at issue. It does not follow that giving criticism in a positive way means that it will necessarily be accepted in the same way. A person may still *take* criticism destructively regardless of the intention with which it is offered. The critic and the

criticized must cooperate if the goal of changed behavior is to be achieved.

In this and the following chapter we have outlined
and developed a basic model for giving and taking
criticism in a positive way. It explains how each of us
can use our thoughts, feelings and actions to make
criticism serve our better purposes. From this model
we derive many specific techniques of constructive
criticism. And in subsequent chapters we explore
these techniques further, to show how they can be
applied when dealing with children, sexual partners,
employers and co-workers, and in self-criticism. Let
us first examine the substance and style of criticism—that is, what to say and how to say it.

What to Say

To offer criticism in a constructive and effective way,
one must answer a series of basic questions. Each
imposes a modest task designed to help the critic
move closer to that goal. The questions involve both
the *content* and the *process* of criticism. Content
questions help to determine *what* information needs
to be communicated. Process questions help to determine *how* to communicate it. Obviously what we say
and how we say it are intertwined; content and process affect each other.

To illustrate how ineffective or damaging criticism
can be converted into helpful and supportive statements, we have chosen three examples of common

critical remarks, each of which represents a different category of personal relationship. Using these criticisms as a guide, we will see how they can become positive instruments for change and growth, despite the limited promise they appear to have at this point.

—*On an intimate level* (spouse to spouse, or lover to lover): "You never consider my feelings." The exact wording isn't important—it may be "You don't pay enough attention to me," or "You don't love me." The meaning of the criticism remains the same.

—*In a work-related setting* (supervisor to subordinate, or employee to colleague): "The trouble with you is, you're too stubborn to change your ways." Again, the exact wording doesn't matter; the same basic criticism can come in many versions.

—*Between friends or acquaintances:* "You don't keep in touch with me anymore. You don't seem to care about our friendship."

All of these remarks are accusatory and hostile; worse, they are pointlessly vague. The first step toward converting them into constructive criticisms is to examine them in terms of "content."

What Do I Want to Criticize?

In determining the specific content of a criticism, you must first ask yourself: *What behavior do I want to criticize?* Once you have thought the answer through you will be able to pinpoint *exactly* what the other person is doing (or failing to do) that bothers you. In the case of the three preceding examples the attempt to become more specific might alter them thus:

You never consider my feelings.	*You say things without thinking how they will affect me,* (or) *You don't show any appreciation for what I do,* (or, more specifically) *You completely forgot our anniversary.*
You're too stubborn to change your ways.	*You claim the new production schedule won't work, but you haven't been willing to give it a real try.*
You don't seem to care about our friendship.	*You haven't called or written in months.*

Pinpointing the specific behavior you want to criticize helps in several ways. For one, it prevents you from making broad generalizations and from adding those hollow and vastly irritating words, "always" and "never." As we noted previously, it is easy for a criticized person to ignore or reject a sweeping statement like those that appear in the first column. He or she can almost always come up with an exception to it. "Didn't I send you flowers on your birthday last year?" "Stubborn? Me? How about the time I went along with that crazy packaging idea?" "You forgot that I sent you a postcard when I was on vacation."

The criticized person can also disagree with the criticism by defining the behavior at issue in a different way. Words like *considerate, stubborn* or *thoughtless* can convey a variety of meanings to different people. When the criticized person can point to an exception, or quibble about meaning, the argument that is likely to follow pushes the criticism itself into the background and deprives it of much of its validity.

When a criticism is presented with precision and accuracy it lets the other person know exactly what you are talking about (and also lets him or her know that *you* know exactly what you are talking about). Your criticism becomes far more credible. Instead of feeling unjustly attacked, the other person is more likely to accept your comment as reasonable, fair and worthy of serious thought. Instead of starting an ill-defined debate or producing a blanket denial, criticism that pinpoints specific behavior is more likely to initiate a constructive two-way dialogue.

Is Change Possible?

Once you have defined the specific behavior you wish to criticize, you must then consider: *Can the criticized behavior be changed?* You are obliged to make an objective assessment of whether or not the other person realistically is able to make the desired change in actions or attitudes. Or, if change is feasible, how likely it is that he or she will agree to it.

In each of the three illustrations we are using, the criticized behavior can be changed. But what if it cannot be changed? It is obviously useless to criticize a man for losing his hair, or to scold a youngster for not getting A's when the child's intellectual capacity makes him a C student. It is perhaps less obvious, but equally useless, for Tom, a highly competitive tennis player, to upbraid his partner, Bill, for playing poorly in a club tournament doubles match. "We lost because you messed up every net shot!" he charges. But Tom knows Bill isn't a top-notch player, especially when it comes to strokes requiring quick reflexes. Bill tries his best but is simply not physically equipped to play any better. Instead of criticizing Bill, Tom needs to ask himself, *Why am I blaming him for our loss? Isn't it as much my fault? After all, I knew how he played when I agreed to be his partner.* Like Tom, many of us criticize to no useful purpose. If one asks, in effect, *Why am I saying these things?* the honest answer may be: *to vent my own annoyance or disappointment.*

And what if someone does not wish to change the criticized behavior? "I once shared an office with a fellow editor whose desk was always a mess," a man said. "I couldn't understand how anyone could work efficiently under those conditions, and I used to nag him about it. But he would say, 'I like it this way. I work better when it's messy, so you might as well save your breath.'" Useless criticism is quickly disregarded as nagging.

Will My Criticism Help?

Still examining the content of your criticism, ask yourself: *How can my criticism contribute to the well-being of the other person, or to an improvement in our relationship?*

Change is motivated by holding out a promise, by specifying the advantage that will accrue to the criti-

cized person. Positive reinforcement—the prospect
of benefit or reward—is a powerful incentive for
change. But criticism is all too often communicated
with a stick rather than a carrot. As a result, it is
heard as a demand, a threat, or an order.

Without the lure of an incentive, criticism seems to
be a command to change for the criticizer's benefit
alone. With an incentive, we give the other person a
reason to change for his or her own advantage. This
helps him or her to break through the barrier of defensiveness most of us automatically erect against
criticism. The incentive serves to convert what we
would ordinarily take to be a put-down as a possible
"put-up."

How does this affect our original three examples?

*You never consider
my feelings.*

*You say things without thinking
how they may make me feel,
you don't appreciate what I do
for you, you even forgot our anniversary. But if you stopped to
consider my feelings, if you
thought to give me a small sign
of love once in a while, I would
feel you really cared about me.
And I would want to do even
more for you. If I felt more appreciated life would be so much
more pleasant for both of us. I
wouldn't always complain and
you wouldn't feel I was nagging
you all the time.*

In this case the incentive is primarily interpersonal:
we will have a better relationship. There is also a

secondary incentive that is wholly personal so far as the criticized partner is concerned: you will feel less put-upon.

The second example provides an illustration of strong personal incentives:

You're too stubborn to change your ways.	*You claim the new schedule won't work, but you aren't giving it a fair chance. If you did, you might find it works much better than you think. And if that is so, your job will be much easier. You'll have time to get more involved with management decisions rather than confining yourself to production problems. That could open a whole new dimension in your career with the company. And it would show the big boss how flexible you can be when you want to.*

The last example can now be rephrased to tone down the accusation of insensitivity and to provide both personal and interpersonal incentives for a more rewarding relationship:

You don't seem to care about our friendship.	*You haven't been keeping in touch with me lately, and it makes me wonder if you still value our friendship. If I knew it was as meaningful to you as it is to me, I could put more time and energy into it. For instance, I'm making travel plans*

> *for next summer. I'd like to in-*
> *clude you in them if you want*
> *to join me.*

All of these revised criticisms provide a stimulus for changed behavior. But what if the person we are criticizing isn't impressed by the offer? What if he or she doesn't think it is worth making any changes?

People do have different value systems, and one person's incentive may be no spur at all to another. To guard against such miscalculation it is essential that the incentive you offer be based on what you believe the *other person* would consider a valuable inducement to change—not what *you* would consider a motivating pay-off.

For example, a spouse's promise to "do more for you" might not be too important a consideration to the unappreciative spouse—he or she might feel that would only lead to demands for *more* appreciation; but "less nagging" might be very important. The employee might not give much of a hoot about whether he was considered flexible, but might welcome the chance to be involved in management decisions. Sensing what is most significant to the criticized person can help you differentiate between effective and ineffective incentives to change.

What New Behavior Do I Wish to See?

If you believe that the behavior of the person you wish to criticize can in fact change, you must then determine: *What do I want the person I am criticizing actually to do?*

Criticism often proves ineffective because by concentrating on what the other person has done "wrong," it fails to state clearly what it is we would like him or her to do "right." That's one reason why negative criticism frequently leaves us feeling we haven't solved anything, haven't made our point. One of the failings frequently mentioned by people who wish to improve the form and content of their criticisms is: "I realized later that I hadn't said what I had wanted to."

Knowing—and stating—just what you want the criticized person to do, or how you want him or her to behave, compels you to think your criticism through. "Must you drive like that?" is sloppy criticism. It conveys nothing except annoyance with what the driver is doing; it offers no clue as to what the criticizer wants the driver to do. Go slower, or faster? Brake less suddenly? Stop weaving from lane to lane? Keep two hands on the wheel?

Or consider the harried wife who says to her husband, "How can you sit there watching television when the house is a mess and company is coming?" That criticism is not likely to produce any action. To be effective, she should make the same point by suggesting specific things the man could do: "Company will be here soon. Could you help me set the table (move the chairs, put the roast in the oven, tidy up the mess in the living room)?"

A second constructive result of incorporating specific suggestions into criticism is that it generates new approaches to a problem. If others fail to respond constructively it is usually not because they don't want to, but because they are not clear about what you have in mind. This is especially true in situations involving work subordinates and children.

Telling an employee, "Your conduct in this office is just not up to company standards" will not produce useful change. But outlining specifically what he or she can do to resolve the problem—stop gossiping with other workers, quit playing office politics—minimizes the possibility that the employee won't know which standards you are referring to, and how to meet them.

Similarly, "You'll drop that glass of milk if you carry it like that" is no help to a young child who isn't sure how you think the glass should be carried. How much better to say, "Hold your glass in two hands," or "Put the sandwich down until you've carried the glass to the table."

"A true critic," wrote the English essayist Joseph Addison, "ought to dwell rather upon excellencies than imperfections." For example, shortly after moving to a new town a woman complained to a neighbor about the poor service at the local drugstore. She hoped the neighbor would repeat her criticism to the owner. The next time she went to the store the druggist greeted her with a smile, said he hoped she liked the town, and asked her to let him know if he could do anything to help her get settled. He then filled her order promptly and efficiently. The woman later reported this changed behavior to her neighbor. "I suppose you told the druggist what I said?" she asked. "Well, no," the neighbor replied. "I hope you don't mind, but I told him you thought it was one of the best-managed drugstores you ever saw."

Communicating what we like or want rather than focusing on what we don't like or want evokes positive responses. Moreover, accentuating the positives often makes it possible to avoid mentioning the negative altogether.

Let's see how this approach changes our original three examples. Notice how in each revised version the critic avoids harping on what's wrong and concentrates on what he or she would prefer the other person to do.

You never consider my feelings.	*I'd like it if you showed an interest in how my day goes, notice the little things I do for you, bring me flowers occasionally. It is important for me to feel you care about me, because I love you very much. I would like to know you sometimes think of me when we're apart. I'd feel more appreciated, and certainly more loving toward you. And you would probably feel less nagged.*
You're too stubborn to change your ways.	*I would like you to try to implement the new schedule, see how it goes. It could make our jobs easier and give you more time to work in the management area. I think you would find a whole new dimension to your career here. It would certainly show the big boss you have the qualities for promotion.*

You don't seem to care about our friendship.	*I wish you'd let me hear from you more often. I like you, and I like being friends with you. Our friendship is really important to me. A phone call or a letter from time to time would let me know that you feel the same way. If I knew our friendship meant as much to you as it does to me, I'd be willing to put even more time and energy into it. For instance, maybe I could plan a trip for both of us next summer.*

Is My Criticism Understood?

Finally, you must ask yourself: *Does the criticized person understand what I am saying? Does he or she agree or disagree with me?* It's important to make sure that the other person is not merely hearing your words, but also interpreting them accurately. Otherwise he or she may draw faulty conclusions.

"You don't appreciate me," or "You aren't considerate of my feelings" may be a plea for closeness between partners. But an insecure spouse may interpret it as meaning, "I can't take this kind of marriage any longer and I'm going to leave you." The employee criticized for being "set in his ways" may interpret that to mean "I don't think you can do your job properly."

The simplest way to make sure the criticized person does comprehend your meaning, is to ask: "Do you understand what I'm saying?" or, "What do you think I am trying to tell you?" Any question will do that obliges the other person to repeat the substance of the criticism as he or she understands it.

We all have a strong tendency to believe that the meaning we give to someone else's words or gestures is accurate. Yet frequently it is not the meaning the speaker intended. A family counselor tells of a particularly critical husband who was in the habit of coldly and silently shrugging his shoulders in reply to his wife's questions. The therapist asked what the shrug meant. "Before he could answer," the counselor recalls, "his wife quickly said, 'I know what it means. He's telling me I've done something wrong again, and as far as he's concerned I can go to hell.' But when the man finally had a chance to speak he said the shrug meant, 'I really don't know how to answer the question because I've never thought about it before.' "

It is also useful to ask the person you are criticizing if he or she agrees or disagrees with the criticism. At the least this precludes a silent or sullen reaction; whatever the response, a dialogue has been started. Being criticized makes many people feel attacked or defenseless. If they are encouraged (or permitted) to express an opinion about the criticism, this feeling can to some extent be dispelled.

Checking for agreement or disagreement prevents the critic from making false assumptions and having faulty expectations. Taking for granted that the other person concurs with the criticism frequently leads to the belief that he or she will take steps to act upon it.

If the expected behavior change does not occur, the critic is upset and disappointed.

How to Say It

In order to offer criticism that will be constructive and effective you need to explore questions concerning "process" as well as content—not just *what* you say, but *how you say it*.

Opinion versus Fact

In deciding how to phrase a critical remark, first ask yourself: *Am I communicating my criticism in such a way that the other person will be most receptive to it?*

Almost everyone experiences at least a twinge of resistance or resentment when being criticized. Yet when the shoe is on the other foot—when we are the critic—we expect others to accept our words readily and to interpret them as well meant. That, plus a touch of defensiveness about being critical, accounts for the frequent use of such disclaimers as, "I'm only telling you this for your own good."

It is not in human nature to feel appreciative or receptive when having one's flaws pointed out, even when the comments are supposed to be helpful. The best you can do, then, is to try to convince the other person of your constructive intentions. Saying "This is for your own good" is hardly the way to accomplish this. More important than any words is the context in which you say them.

Make it clear that you realize your criticism is not necessarily a statement of fact, but simply a reflection of your opinion. Criticisms are neither true nor false in and of themselves. Most critical comment is a judgment, an evaluation based on your personal perceptions and beliefs: "You behaved rudely when the Websters came to visit." "That hairstyle looks dreadful on you." "If you had any tact you'd have gotten that promotion." All these remarks reflect *opinions*; others might judge that same behavior, hairstyle or personal temperament differently.

Voicing criticism as a factual statement immediately puts the other person on the defensive. He or she is almost forced to rebut with negative argument: "I did not behave rudely." "I think my hair looks nice." "I'm not going to toady to anyone for a better job."

If you communicate criticism as your individual perception of a situation, others are going to be more willing to listen—and may even be curious as to why you saw it as you did. In essence, you are giving them the chance to compare their ideas and feelings with yours. The result is more likely to be a constructive dialogue than a useless exchange of charges and defenses.

How do you frame your criticism as a perception rather than a fact? By using "I" statements and subjective phrases: "In my opinion, you behaved rudely last night." "I may not be up on the latest styles, but I don't think that hairdo flatters you." "The way I see it, you might have gotten that promotion if you had been more diplomatic."

There is another reason why such "I" statements

and self-referent phrases are effective. They help the critic to be more responsible for his or her criticism. If we are clear that what we are saying may be true only for ourselves, we are likely to choose our words more carefully. This helps to eliminate broad generalizations and accusations.

The Empathy Factor

In considering the impact your words may have, ask yourself: *Am I expressing my criticism in a way that shows I understand the other person's feelings?*

If you feel sorry for someone, you are being *sympathetic* to his or her feelings. If you can put yourself in another's place well enough to feel sorry "with" that person—to share temporarily the same reactions, to anticipate the emotional response—you are displaying *empathy*.

As adults we seem more able to be empathetic with children than with other adults. When a youngster is disappointed because rain has wiped out a long-anticipated picnic, or a day at the baseball game, we understand exactly how the child feels. We identify emotionally with that disappointment. When an adult's plans are disrupted we may sympathize but we don't usually empathize. Perhaps we believe grown-ups ought to be able to handle disappointment without our emotional support.

It's not hard to be empathetic when the feelings you are trying to understand are similar to those you might feel in a similar situation. But empathy is harder to achieve when the other person's reaction challenges what you consider to be a "truth." (That is another reason to remember that your criticisms are not necessarily truths.)

Empathy can be communicated, directly and indirectly, via feelings, thoughts and actions. When you are criticizing someone, check your "empathy quotient" in these three areas:

If I were the other person, how would I feel if he or she said this to me?   If being on the receiving end of the criticism would make you angry or resentful, look for the words or tones that triggered those feelings and try to present your criticism in a different way. "The genius of communication," writes philosopher John Powell, "is the ability to be both totally honest and totally kind at the same time."

If I were the other person, what would I think if he or she said this to me?   The answer to this question will help you decide if you are making your point in a constructive way. Would you think you were going to lose the criticizer's affection or respect? Would you think you were being picked on unfairly? Would you think a mountain was being made out of a molehill? If the criticism produces these counterproductive inferences in your mind, most likely it is having the same sort of effect on the other person. You need to rephrase your remarks to minimize these negative implications.

If I were the other person, would I appreciate being criticized at this moment, or in this situation?   How would you feel if you were censured in front of classmates or colleagues? How would you react if your spouse found fault with your appearance in front of friends or guests? How would you like to be blamed for a mistake the minute you came home from work? Choosing the appropriate time and place to offer criticism is one way of behaving empathetically.

Commitment to the Criticism

Before offering even the smallest criticism, it is important to ask yourself: *Am I committed to the criticism I am making? Do I see it as part of a continuing process?*

Too often we deliver a criticism and then forget about it. The criticized person is left to dangle, feeling helpless, perhaps victimized, certainly undirected. Assuming, with some reason, that nothing further will be said or done, he or she may conclude, "I guess that's the end of it, so I'll just forget the whole thing."

If your criticism is going to produce a constructive response, you need to show that you are committed not only to what you have said, but also to fostering the changed behavior you hope will follow. You must show you care about the matter and are willing to cooperate in dealing with it. To put it still another way, constructive criticism seeks to form an alliance between giver and taker in order to reach their common goal.

For example, a general remark such as "That's not a good idea" is only the barest beginning of a criticism. To have any useful effect it must be accompanied by explanations and suggestions showing why it isn't a good idea and what sort of approach would be more feasible.

A young woman executive recalls being told by her superior, after a month on the job, that she was spending too much time on unimportant tasks. "He just said that to me and walked away. I didn't know what to do, because I didn't know what he considered unimportant, or what he wanted me to concentrate on. Worse yet, he never said another word about it. For months I went about my job in perpetual fear that I was going to be fired for incompetence."

How do you show you are committed to your criticism? By making your comments specific; by offering suggestions or solutions that may remedy the situation; and by making it a point to tell the person you are criticizing that you know he or she is trying to resolve the matter and has (or has not yet) made a change for the better. This interaction is vital to the success of the critical process, for it indicates that you are trying to help and are willing to be supportive. If you are not committed to your criticism you might as well not offer it at all; without any follow-up on your part it is unlikely to be productive.

The Effect of Attitude

The way you present your criticism is bound to be affected by these considerations: *Am I aware of my own feelings when I criticize someone? Are they positive or negative?*

If your feelings as you offer criticism are hostile, anxious or punitive, they are bound to color your remarks. A negative attitude is difficult to conceal, and the other person is apt to react to your emotional attitude rather than to the substance of your words.

But the motive behind a criticism is not always easy to identify. An unemployed man, for instance, may be overly critical of his wife and children. In actuality he is finding fault with them because he needs to bolster his lowered self-esteem and knows no other way to do so. He salves his own wounds by wounding others.

Motives can usually be discerned by the circumstances in which the criticism is given. It is one thing to tell your wife, while she is getting ready for a dinner party, that the dress she plans to wear is unbecoming. Your motive then may be to save her from embarrassment, or to help her look more attractive. It is quite another matter to make that criticism just as you are about to enter the host's home. In that case the motive is more likely to be a hostile one.

A Criticism Model

Now that we have shown how "content" and "process" questions can help you change potentially destructive criticism into potentially constructive and effective criticism, let's look at how those factors might be incorporated into the three examples we have been using. Here they are in final form. The words in parentheses identify the specific content or process factor that applies to the preceding sentence.

You never consider my feelings.

I'd really like it if you would show me that you notice the things I do for you, or if you sometimes brought me flowers or some other sign of appreciation and love. (Specific pinpointing of criticism accompanied by statement of what you would like the other person to do about it.) *I realize you may feel that you do show me that you care about me, but I feel I don't get enough of that.* (Criticism as opinion; I-statements.) *This is important to me because I love you very much and I need to know that you think about me and care about what happens in my life.* (Expressing personal feelings.) *If you changed, I would certainly feel more loving toward you* (I-statements and incentive to change), *and you would probably feel less nagged.* (Incentive.) *I know I've said all this before and you must be tired of hearing it, and probably frustrated too.* (Empathy.) *Maybe you feel that you show love in ways that I don't recognize—and you probably do.* (Empathy again.) *So I have a suggestion to make: I'll always tell you how much I appreciate it when I'm aware that you have done something to show your love for me, or when you point out to me that you have.* (Commitment to interaction.) *I think this whole thing is important to us as a couple.* (Expressing own feelings.) *I'd like you to tell me what you think so I can be sure you understand exactly what I have been trying to say.* (Getting agreement.)

You're too stubborn to change your ways.

I believe you could add a whole new dimension to your work by being more innovative in your job. (I-statement; incentive.) *You could begin to do this by putting the new production schedule into effect.* (Pinpointing.) *I'd be pleased if you did because it would make both our jobs easier, and give you more time to develop your own ideas.* (Incentive; stating criticizer's own needs.) *I know you're reasonably satisfied with the way things are going now, and I also know it's not easy to change the system overnight.* (Empathy.) *But I wish you would think seriously about what I've said, and then maybe in a week or two we can talk about how to*

initiate the changes effectively.
(Commitment to interaction.)
*How do you feel about what
I've been saying?* (Validation of
criticism.)

*You don't seem to
care about our
friendship.*

*I like being your friend, and you
know our friendship is important to me.* (Expressing positive
feelings.) *But I'm wondering if
it is as important to you, because it seems to me you
haven't written or called in a
long time.* (I-statement; criticism
expressed as perception; criticism pinpointed.) *I know how
busy you are* (empathy), *but a
phone call or a brief note from
time to time would make me
feel good.* (Suggestions for re-
medial action.) *It would encourage me to give more of myself to
our relationship.* (Incentive.)
What do you think? (Validation.)

By tracing the evolution of a criticism from an
offhand comment, negative in tone and ineffective in
content, to a well-planned statement that is both effective and positive, we have outlined the structure
of a model for constructive criticism. Reduced to its
essential framework, the model serves to sharpen the
focus of a criticism and make it productive for both
giver and receiver:

    1.   What behavior do I want to change?

2.   Can this behavior be changed?

3.   What do I want my criticism to accomplish for me/us?

4.   Am I expressing empathy with the person I am criticizing?

5.   Is the criticism being offered in an appropriate environment?

Here are some examples of the model in action, drawn from actual experiences of students in our criticism workshops. It is important to remember that not every negative factor needs to be present in order for a criticism to be destructive, nor does every positive factor need to be present to ensure effective criticism.

Burt and Laura had dated several times. Laura liked Burt's quick mind and good looks, but was put off by his social behavior, for while she tended to be quiet and retiring, he was loud and enjoyed being the center of attention.

One evening, while having dinner with a group of Laura's friends, Burt loudly talked about his accomplishments and his opinions, often interrupting other speakers and shouting over their words. Laura felt embarrassed and ashamed of Burt. By the time dessert was served she was furious with him.

"Will you shut up?" she said suddenly. "Must you be such a loudmouth? You are always interrupting! My friends and I like to have a conversation, too. You've managed to ruin the evening!"

The destructive aspects of Laura's tirade should be obvious: the shaming words ("shut up," "loudmouth," "ruined the evening"); the generalization ("always"); the inappropriate environment; and the absence of any attempt to understand Burt's problem.

When Laura was able to apply the criticism model to the situation in which she found herself, she reasoned that:

1. The specific behavior that she wanted to help change—Burt's habit of rudely interrupting—could probably be changed.

2. Her criticism could help Burt by pointing out a flaw in his personality he may not have realized exists. Overcoming it would improve his relationships in general and with Laura in particular.

3. By saying what she did, when she did, she had been hostile instead of empathetic.

This analysis enabled Laura to adopt a different criticism strategy. The next time Burt's loudness in public annoyed her, Laura waited until they were driving home together. Then she said:

"Burt, we've dated several times now, and you know I enjoy being with you. But I'd enjoy it a lot more—and like you much better—if you didn't try to dominate the conversation all the time. I like to talk without being interrupted, and so do my friends. And it embarrasses me when you are so loud. I'd appreciate it if you would speak more quietly, and let others have their

turn. I know that breaking into conversations may just be a habit you picked up, a habit that is hard for you to break. But I'll try to help you by winking at you if you start to interrupt someone. Okay?"

In this version, Laura emphasized the positive aspects of her criticism. If Burt changed, she would like him better, their dates would be more pleasant, and breaking the habit would help Burt in his other relationships as well. Instead of accusations, Laura used I-statements to make it plain that these were her subjective feelings. She understood that it may be hard for Burt to change, but committed herself to a continuing effort to help him do so. And she drew him into a constructive discussion of the problem by asking for his response to her criticism.

In another case, a class of student-teachers gathered to hear the comments of their supervisor. The latter glanced at his notes and then singled out a rather nervous young man. In the first paragraph is the supervisor's original criticism; on the next page is the revised version.

Ted, your performance is extremely disappointing. You don't seem to take the job or your responsibilities seriously. For instance, whenever a youngster misbehaved in class, or gave an incorrect answer to a question, you began to laugh. (Ted tries to explain but the supervisor continues in a harsh voice.) *Maybe you should think twice about your ability and motivation to teach. I know I will, so you had better shape up!*

Ted, I noticed that you laughed a lot in your class today. Now, humor and laughter can be an excellent way to create rapport with youngsters. But I believe it is more effective if you laugh with them rather than at them. It may be worth your while to think about how you can incorporate a sense of humor into your teaching skills. There have been several articles on that topic in education journals. If you like, I'll dig some out of my files and discuss them with you.

The original criticism took Ted to task in front of his peers, used generalizations and threats, did not suggest specific action for change, and closed off with a threat, eliminating any opportunity for discussion or follow-up. In the revised version—delivered in the privacy of the supervisor's office—criticism was offered as a stepping stone to increased professional skill. And instead of cutting off discussion with a threat, the supervisor left the door open for change by offering to help Ted.

The two preceding examples showed how the criticism model can be used to convert negative criticism into positive criticism. But the model can also help to generate constructive criticism from scratch. In one workshop session a woman named Carla explained her problem:

As program chairperson of my Community Affairs Club, I'm responsible for getting guest speakers for our monthly meeting. I enjoy the assignment because I get to meet many interesting men and women in our town. But there is one pesky fly in the ointment. One of our members insists on asking contentious questions in a belligerent way. She attacks the speaker, sometimes breaking right into the speech. It's dreadfully embarrassing to me, to our guests, and to other members. But this woman has been a hardworking club member for years; as a matter of fact she is a former president. I don't want to alienate her but I have to get her to see what she is doing, and to stop it.

Through a series of leading questions Carla was helped to build her criticism around the framework of the model.

"What specific behavior do you want to criticize?"

"Her asking those questions," Carla said.

"Can you be more specific? Any questions, or certain ones?"

"Well, just the ones that are impertinent or unnecessarily provoking," she replied. "And the ones that interrupt the speaker."

"Do you think the woman can successfully change this behavior?"

"Of course I do," said Carla.

"And if she did, just how would it help everyone concerned?"

"Obviously our meetings would be more pleasant," Carla said. "And it would ease my task in getting other guests. Holding all questions till the speaker is through would make for a more stimulating discussion period. And to be honest, I think the other members would not resent this woman as much as they do now."

"*What exactly would you like this woman to do?*"

"Well, as I said, to hold her questions until the end, and to be more diplomatic when she asks them."

"*How would you think it best to say these things to her?*"

"I think I ought to do it face to face rather than on the telephone," Carla said. "And I'd want to do it privately, just the two of us. The best time would probably be just before our next meeting."

Based on this Socratic dialogue, Carla spoke this way to the troublesome member the following month:

> *Norma, you know we all appreciate your participation in meetings. However, it strikes some of the women—and me—that our guests sometimes react defensively to many of the questions you ask, especially when you challenge them. I think your questions could be much more productive if you held them for the question period at the end.*
>
> *I know it's hard to wait, particularly if you have what you think is a really pertinent point to make. I often feel that urge to break in, myself. But it would be more effective, and more gracious, if you could wait. I'd really appreciate your thinking about this. By the way, if you have a good question and are afraid you might forget it, perhaps you could write it down. From now*

on I'm going to have pads and pencils available for every member.

CHECKLIST FOR CONSTRUCTIVE CRITICISM:

1. Target the behavior you want to criticize.
2. Make your criticism as specific as possible.
3. Be sure the behavior you are criticizing can be changed. If it cannot, then stop.
4. Use "I-statements" and avoid threats and/or accusations.
5. Make sure the other person understands your criticism and the reason for it. Don't mumble or talk too fast. Even the best of criticism is useless if the other person does not grasp what you are saying.
6. Don't belabor the point. Lengthy and repeated criticism simply inspires the other person to "tune out." Similarly, don't turn your criticism into a lecture; bored listeners pay no attention.
7. Offer incentives for changed behavior, and commit yourself to share in resolving the situation.
8. Don't allow your own negative feelings to color your words. Watch your voice for overtones of hostility or sarcasm. Avoid angry gestures such as clenched fists, scowls and frowns, or pointing fingers. Nonverbal attitudes should reinforce your words, not contradict them.
9. Show that you empathize with the other person's problem or feelings.
10. Hold criticism for an appropriate time and place. Spontaneous criticism may lead you to say things you don't really mean, or to express yourself in a destructive way.

11.   Consider trying to defuse a hostile response to criticism by "predicting" the other person's reaction: "I know I can say this to you because I know you will take it well."

12.   If your criticism produces positive results, give verbal recognition and appreciation.

4 | How to Take Criticism and Profit by It

Not long ago a team of sex therapists leveled a sharp attack on the research methods used by Drs. William Masters and Virginia Johnson, the famed pioneers in the treatment of sexual response. The critique—published in an important national magazine—attacked almost every phase of their work. When Masters and Johnson were offered the chance to reply to the charges they politely declined, stating that it was not their policy to reply to criticism in any popular forum.

Most people would like to be able to react to criticism that calmly, but few can. Their defenses are triggered and they react angrily, thus assuring the critic that he has touched a sore spot, or they respond resentfully, thereby making it difficult to build any bridges of communication. Yet while no one likes to be criticized, learning how to accept criticism in a confident way enables it to help rather than hurt.

You have probably been told more than once that you should "take criticism constructively." But rarely is anyone told exactly *how* to do this best. For the most part, accepting criticism constructively has traditionally meant curbing your irritation, making believe your feelings have not been hurt, or even falsely agreeing with the critic. But calling upon such negative and emotionally damaging responses is hardly the way to take a positive stance.

Rather, accepting criticism in a constructive way means learning to use it as a catalyst for personal growth—as an opportunity to make choices rather than to accede to demands. To accomplish this you must develop skills that will give that familiar trio— thoughts, feelings and actions—the power to work for you, not against you. Specifically, you must:

—Think of criticism as a source of new information to be evaluated objectively;

—Channel the emotional energy aroused by criticism into fruitful avenues; and

—Take the necessary steps to put behavioral changes into action.

Judging Criticism

We talked earlier about the importance of appraisal in dealing with criticism, and how most people tend to appraise it negatively. But since the way we appraise critical remarks determines how we react to them, and since how we react in turn affects how we appraise them, what's required is a new kind of strategy for judging the soundness, cogency and worth of a criticism.

A first step is to examine the criticism in terms of its new, positive definition. For example, when psychologists asked several men and women to finish the statement, "When I am criticized, . . ." one said, "I try to figure out why. Maybe the other fellow sees things differently than I do. It's not that either of us is right or wrong." A woman replied, "I listen carefully. Criticism tells me much about the criticizer—how she thinks, what she expects." Another woman said, "I realize how others are seeing me." When we evaluate criticism from this point of view we can begin to tune in to the information it has to offer us rather than let that information turn us off.

A second step is to change the tenor of the statements we make to ourselves when we are criticized. This "private speech" is often a major factor in the way we appraise criticism. A sociologist asked hundreds of men and women to record what goes on in their minds when they receive criticism. Here are some of the self-statements they most frequently mentioned.

—*I didn't realize it was going to be this bad.*
—*He's going to fire me, that's what's coming next.*
—*She doesn't love me anymore.*
—*When will he be finished talking?*
—*I can't take this. I've got to get away.*
—*Boy, do I have answers for her!*

Significantly, not one of these self-statements has anything to do with the specific content of the criticism that provoked it. Nor does any of them deal with the criticism in a realistic way. They are, in effect, merely instructions to oneself to be worried, angry, afraid, hostile. To appraise criticism constructively depends on one's ability to shift to positive private speech. For example:

—*I don't have to prove myself. This isn't an attack on me.*

—*Listen carefully. What she is saying may be helpful.*

—*Try to find out what this person wants so you won't repeat the mistake.*

—*Stay relaxed. There's no need to argue.*

There are several ways you can change the tone of self-statements:

Alter your belief system. Self-statements are generated by belief systems. *Criticism means I failed* is an example of a faulty system that perpetuates negative self-statements. One way of changing a belief system is to appraise criticism more accurately.

Change your style of thinking. Many people use thought processes—overgeneralization, "either-or" reasoning—that help to produce negative self-statements. By being aware of how you think about a criticism you can, for example, change *This person always criticizes me* to *This person criticizes me some of the time.* Similarly, either-or reasoning will lead you to tell yourself *I did a bad thing* or *I did not do anything bad.* Changing that style of thinking about criticism can help you to say, instead, *Some things I did were bad, but others were not.*

Examine your self-statements to become aware of how often you use negative ones. By increasing the number of positive self-statements you make to yourself, you will begin to implement more constructive actions. It may seem like basic logic to say that negative self-statements are incompatible with positive ones, but the fact is that as you voice and act upon positive self-statements, you will find yourself voicing fewer negative ones.

Appraising Specific Criticisms

Should you promptly move to change your behavior whenever you are criticized? Not at all. Criticism should first be used as a cue that it *may* be time to take some positive steps. The process of appraisal helps you judge whether a criticism is sufficiently valid to warrant your acting on it. If you decide it is not valid, or that you cannot benefit from it, refuse it in a constructive way. (We shall talk later in this chapter about how to do this.) But if you decide the criticism is valid, then it is time to use it as a source of energy for change.

Before you can appraise the validity of a criticism, you must make sure you are interpreting it accurately.

Interpreting the Specific Criticism

Analyze what the specific criticism means to you and how you interpret it.

Scott, a graduate biochemistry student, was crushed when his report on a lab experiment was labeled "sloppy and incomplete."

"I couldn't accept that," Scott said. "Even though I knew I hadn't been as thorough as I should have, I argued with my professor. But I really wasn't thinking about the report. All that went through my mind was, 'You idiot, now you're going to fail this course and flunk out!' That's what the criticism said to me—that I was a rotten scientist and probably would never get my Ph.D."

After long and futile argument Scott finally admitted he had skimped on some key parts of his experiment. To his surprise, the teacher then responded with helpful suggestions rather than the caustic comments Scott had expected.

Scott, of course, had interpreted the criticism in the conventional destructive way: "Grad school is terribly competitive, and when you're told you are doing a poor job it means you are in real trouble." As a result it was difficult for Scott to look beyond the surface of the criticism and ask himself, *What is the professor really trying to tell me?*

To evaluate a specific criticism accurately you should ask such questions not only of yourself but of the criticizer as well. In Scott's case the professor was not telling him he was about to fail, but reminding him that he needed to work up to his higher capacity. Scott needed to make sure he was interpreting the criticism correctly rather than jump to a stereotyped conclusion. Remember, as your evaluation of general criticism becomes more productive, your appraisal of specific criticism will tend to be more accurate.

There are six basic guidelines by which you can appraise the validity of a criticism.

Importance of Criticism

After you have appraised the specific criticism accurately, you must then ask yourself: *How important is this criticism (piece of information)?* The answer to this question will be a significant determinant in helping you decide if you want to take action to resolve it.

For example, a salesman stated that every time he had a meeting with his supervisor, he would be criticized for wearing "mod" clothing. "You've got to dress more conservatively if you want to make sales," he was told. However, the salesman did all his selling over the phone and never even met his customers. He saw little merit in his supervisor's criticism. He judged it to be unimportant and continued his style of dressing. However, when the salesman was transferred to another position which involved meeting customers, he reappraised his supervisor's criticism and judged it to be very important. As a result, he dressed more conservatively.

Appraising the importance of a specific criticism will be facilitated when you take into consideration the other guidelines. Thus it is essential to note that the importance of a criticism is not fixed; rather it is free to vary depending on your own needs, the needs of others, and the context in which it is given. But remember, the more important you judge the criticism to be, the more likely it is that you will do something about it.

Assessing the Source

Assess the source of a criticism. Is the critic qualified to judge your attitude or behavior by reason of training or skill? Does he or she know you well enough or long enough to be able to base an opinion on a wealth of experience or an accumulation of fact, rather than on an isolated incident?

We often react poorly to criticism because we feel it is unjust. It is natural to be irritated when you believe the person criticizing you doesn't know what he or she is talking about. For example, a poolside acquaintance remarks that you aren't doing the crawl stroke correctly, and you know he is barely able to dog-paddle. Or your brother-in-law, who consistently loses money in the stock market, says you don't know how to manage your investments wisely. There is no point in becoming upset or defensive; simply ignore the criticism as coming from an invalid source. If you must reply, ask quietly—not angrily or sarcastically—"How do you think I should do it?" or "What are your suggestions?"

Of course your poolside acquaintance may turn out to be a former swimming champion; but assessing the validity of most sources of criticism is not so easy. The task is often confused by overlapping emotional contradictions. Consider Diane, an up-and-coming fashion designer, whose husband Roger, a commercial photographer, incessantly criticized her work.

Roger never liked anything I did. He used to tell me I didn't have enough creativity or imagination to be a designer. His criticisms just crushed me. Imagine, the most important person in my life telling me over and over that I wasn't any good at my work. I didn't want to believe him, but then I figured that Roger was a creative artist too, in his own way, and he must have known what he was talking about.

I actually reached the point of telling my boss that I was thinking of leaving the design field because I felt I could never succeed in it. My boss was stunned. "Where did you get that idea?" he asked. When I told him about Roger's criticisms, he said, "Your husband may be a great guy but he doesn't know beans about fashion design. Your work is on a par with the best in the field."

For a while I didn't know who to believe, my boss or Roger. But I gradually realized I'd been letting my love and respect for Roger dictate my surrender to his criticisms. That was a real turning point. From then on I never let Roger's remarks about my work affect me because I knew he wasn't qualified to comment on it. Once, when he found fault with a drawing I was working on, I asked him how he would design it. He tried a few sketches, but they were clearly off the mark. After that he seemed to be more appreciative of my work. At any rate, the criticisms stopped.

Diane had made the mistake of allowing her emotional involvement with her husband to lend false credibility to his criticism.

In another instance a writer asked an editor friend to read a chapter of a novel he was working on. "My friend was sharply critical of it," the writer said. "He explained that he was being 'brutally frank' only in my best interests. Ordinarily I might have taken his comment at face value. But I knew my friend had failed in his one attempt to write a novel, and I believed that much of his criticism stemmed from hidden jealousy."

To assess the source of a criticism effectively, you must be able to calculate the critic's possible motives. Does he or she want to impress you (or impress those who may be listening) with his or her superior knowledge? Does the critic want to feel superior? Throw his weight around? Intimidate you? Goad you?

When you aren't sure of a critic's motives, consensual validation is a useful technique for sorting out just how legitimate a criticism may be. For instance, if your boss accuses you of being late for work more times than not, you may feel he is nit-picking or exaggerating. But you can't entirely dismiss the charge because you know you're always rushing to try to get to the office on time. In that case, ask co-workers if they feel you are usually late for work; ask friends whether you are frequently late for appointments with them. If both groups agree that punctuality is not your forte, you may assume the boss's criticism is probably valid—that the problem lies with your habitual tardiness rather than with his perception of it.

Gauging the Emotional Climate

Gauge the emotional climate in which the criticism occurs. Lashing out at whomever happens to be nearby is unfortunately one way some people react to their own stress. Thus someone may criticize you merely because he or she is under emotional tension:

> *Jack got home from the office at 6:30 to find that dinner would not be ready at the usual time because the plumber had had to turn off the gas for two hours to fix a leak. The roast his wife Marge was preparing wouldn't be ready until after eight o'clock. Jack exploded.*
>
> *"Why couldn't you have called the plumber this morning instead of waiting till this afternoon? If you knew the gas was going to be off why didn't you just have a salad? But no—you never think ahead!"*
>
> *Marge was surprised by the outburst; Jack did not usually care when they had dinner. Wisely, she surmised that his criticism had another cause. Her suspicions were confirmed when Jack said he planned to eat quickly because he had to work all evening on a report that was due first thing the next day. "Thanks to you I won't even get started till nine!" he grumbled.*

Marge realized that her husband's criticisms were not really aimed at her, but were a by-product of the work pressure he was under, and of his own rigid scheduling. Using "private speech," she told herself that Jack was upset and didn't mean what he had said. So instead of reacting angrily, she overlooked his complaints. "Why don't you relax while dinner's cooking?" she suggested. "I'll make you a drink, and we'll talk, and the roast will be ready before you know it. It will do you good to take a break before you get back to your paperwork."

Chris had been highly praised for the work she had done during her six months as a copy trainee in an advertising agency. Her copy chief had virtually promised her a regular job when the probationary period ended.

Late one Friday afternoon Chris went to her boss's office to turn in the copy for a new account. She put it on his desk just as he received a phone call from the agency vice-president. From her boss's expression Chris realized he was being chewed out. "Well, at least he'll be pleased to get my copy," she thought.

But when the boss slammed down the phone he turned on Chris with a growl. "Don't ever barge into my office like that again!" He glanced at her copy, then tossed it aside. "This stuff is two days late anyway, so what's the big rush? And why is it your stuff is always late, Miss Trainee? You can't expect to get a permanent job here with that kind of record!"

Chris's immediate reaction was anger, followed by hurt. Her copy was never late; she never "barged" into the boss's office. For a moment she was tempted to fight back. "But then I told myself, 'Hold on, Chris. You know you do good work and he knows it, too.' What was happening was that my boss had just been roundly and unfairly criticized by *his* boss, and he was taking out his frustration on me. I figured the best thing to do was to forget the incident, or let him bring it up if he wanted to. Sure enough, he called me in Monday morning and apologized."

Chris's ability to take into account her boss's emotional state enabled her to shrug off his criticisms. But she took the situation still another constructive step forward. "After he apologized," Chris said, "I told him I knew that he'd been upset when he spoke to me that way, so I had not let his scolding get to me. He was grateful for my understanding."

It is not always easy to assess the emotional climate in which criticisms are offered. The incident that triggers a person's need to assail someone else may have occurred hours, days—even years—before. One man recalled how his wife continually criticized and belittled him for no apparent reason. Not until they sought help from a therapist to save their marriage did he discover that it was her unconscious way of taking revenge for a brief extramarital affair he had had—and confessed to—nine years earlier.

If you are aware of emotional contexts you can minimize or even nullify the impact of criticism. But there are times when the emotional context can intensify a criticism, emphasize its seriousness and necessitate a prompt constructive resolution.

"My parents always criticized my driving," said Andrew, 18. *"They said I was reckless, but I didn't think so. Maybe I'd hit the brakes hard, or forget to use the turn signal once in a while—big*

*deal! But whenever they were in the car with me
I'd get a lecture. Well, one day it happened. I
zipped up to a yellow light, hit the brakes at the
last minute—and they didn't hold. I skidded
through the red light and hit another car. No one
was hurt, but both cars were pretty badly banged
up.*

*"Of course my parents were angry. Once they
knew I was okay they laid into me again for the
way I drove. But this time I heard their criticism
in a totally different way. For one thing, I'd been
pretty well shaken up by what happened. I realized there was a point to their criticism. For another, they were deadly serious. There was no
sarcasm, no 'Let's pick on Andy' attitude. They
were concerned that I understand the need to
drive sanely. I guess that's when I decided it was
important to respond to the criticism the same
way they meant it—constructively."*

Repetition of Criticism

Consider the consistency with which a specific criticism is offered. If you are frequently criticized for the
same behavior by a number of different people (or
by the same person), it is a strong indication that the
criticism is valid and should be acted upon.

Appraising criticism on the basis of how consistently it is given may seem much the same as using
consensual validation as a determinant of credibility.
But the two are different. In the latter case you are
trying to establish whether a substantial number of

people agree about the criticized behavior. For example, your colleagues may agree with your employer that you are usually late to work. But they are not criticizing you for that. Consistency means that your co-workers criticize you for lateness just as often as your employer does. Consistency of criticism is significant in that it helps to call our attention to habitual behavior.

Expending "Change Energy"

Estimate how much "change energy" you must expend to correct a criticized behavior. Few things are harder to change than the way we habitually think, feel or act. Some people are unwilling to make the effort; some are too self-centered to adapt to the needs or wishes of others; and some fear what may happen psychologically—a sense of losing control, or of being forced to admit past errors—if they do change. *Things might get better if I change*, they think. *But they could get worse, too. Why risk rocking the boat?*

In any event, it takes emotional energy to make the changes that criticism sometimes demands. And it may seem that you are going to be required to expend more energy than the change is worth. In appraising a specific criticism, therefore, you need to estimate as accurately as possible just *how much* energy you will have to put out in order to correct the attitude or behavior that is at issue.

Bear in mind that when we talk of expending "change energy" we are talking of many varieties of physical or emotional effort. If, for example, a neighbor criticizes the appearance of your lawn and suggests strongly that you do something to improve it, you may feel that good relations are not worth the time and labor necessary to bring the lawn up to your neighbor's standards. If your spouse criticizes you for preferring to watch television rather than go out with friends, you will have to decide whether changing your behavior to meet the objection is worth the social effort involved. If you are criticized by others (or if you fault yourself) for attitudes and actions that prevent you from reaching your goals in life, you will have to decide if you are willing to invest the time and psychic energy involved in undergoing psychotherapy.

Both those who give criticism and those who receive it often erroneously assume that almost any behavior can be changed if a person tries hard enough. But not all the effort in the world can help a person constructively deal with a criticism if it can only be resolved with skills or attributes he does not possess. A student criticized for not being able to grasp the intricacies of calculus will probably never be able to do so, no matter how long he studies, if his mind is not attuned to the abstractions of higher mathematics. No amount of lessons and practice is likely to improve the game of a weekend golfer who does not have the ability to hit better shots. Therefore, be sure that, if you are willing to make the effort to change, there is a reasonable chance to succeed. When continual effort leads only to continual failure, one's self-image suffers doubly. If you sincerely believe that changing is not worth the amount of energy it will take to do so, you have a right to reject the criticism.

Weighing the Pros and Cons

Decide whether the benefits that may accrue from acting on a criticism outweigh (or at least balance) the effort involved. The amount of "change energy" required is only one side of a cost-reward equation. The other is the benefit one may derive from actually changing.

> "My wife has been after me for years to get involved in local politics," said Brian, a middle-aged and highly successful attorney. "She constantly criticizes me, calling me lazy and unambitious, because I won't join the local political club or work for the party in election campaigns. She thinks that if I did, I could eventually be nominated for a city or state office.
>
> "I considered it for a while," Brian went on, "and finally decided the game wasn't worth the candle—not to me, anyway. I find the business of politics wearing, time consuming, and often unpleasant. I'd rather spend my free time with my family, or go off fishing, than go to endless meetings and speeches.
>
> "And even if I did what my wife wanted, and got elected, what would either of us gain? Some influence and prominence, I suppose. But the demands on me would be far greater than they

*are now. I'd probably earn less than I do now.
And I'd be a lot less able to enjoy myself.*

*"Eleanor may think she'd like being the wife
of a councilman, but I bet she'd hate it after a
while. So . . . I'm not going to change and I'm
not going to argue with her. I'm just going to let
her keep calling me unambitious. I think she
will eventually come around to my point of
view."*

If in fact you can see no benefit from acting on a
criticism, or believe it would take too much of a personal investment to change, or if you are satisfied
with things as they are—then by all means you
should feel no obligation to meet a criticism. Problems arise when one reaches that conclusion not because it is authentic and sincere, but because it is
dictated by laziness, by false pride, by rationaliza-
tion, or by other negative factors.

However, it is sometimes difficult to discern the
potential benefits of a criticism unless we are prepared to accept it constructively. Being alert to the
advantages change may offer is in itself an incentive
to positive action, and a source of energy. But your
ability to recognize those advantages often depends
on how the criticism is communicated.

You will recall that in discussing the techniques of
giving constructive criticism we mentioned the importance of offering incentives for change. Many
criticizers, unfortunately, fail to do that. In taking
criticism constructively, therefore, you need to ask
yourself and your critic, "What will I gain?" Your

question should be put in a concerned rather than a hostile manner: "I'm interested in knowing how doing what you suggest will help me." "Can you share with me how you think this will affect us?"

Opening such a dialogue will help each of you to learn the other's motives. And, more important, by focusing the conversation on positives rather than negatives, you will be approaching criticism from the proper perspective.

These six appraisal factors cannot be separated from one another. Each of them—importance, source, emotional context, consistency, energy costs, and potential benefits—interact with one another. All must be taken into consideration in deciding whether a criticism is valid and, if so, whether it is worth doing something to resolve it.

Taking Charge of Emotions

How do I feel when I'm criticized? Terrible! I get a sinking sensation in my stomach, my mouth gets dry, and my breath seems to come in shallow gasps. I feel like I want the words to stop right away.

———

Everything in my body starts racing. My heart beats faster, my face and neck flush and grow hot. I feel a surge of energy—but I don't know what to do with it, and that makes me very edgy.

======

*I feel as if energy is being drained out of me.
Something heavy is unwinding in my stomach,
pulling down the rest of me, but there's no place
for it to go. It takes about an hour for the energy
to return, and during that time I feel exhausted.*

Those are some typical answers people gave when
we asked them to describe the emotions they experience when criticized. Note that in each case they
identify not only a negative *feeling* ("terrible,"
"edgy," "exhausted"), but also a set of bodily
changes. Every emotion is composed of at least these
two elements: on the one hand a variation, either up
or down, in one's level of physiological arousal; and
on the other the label that we attach to that arousal.

The fact is that emotions frequently manifest
themselves in much the same kind of generalized
bodily arousal. It is the label we give to an emotion
that *defines* it for us—tells us whether it is pleasant
or unpleasant. One group of researchers, for example, hooked their subjects to a battery of biofeedback
mechanisms and told them to recall or to visualize an
experience that made them angry. Their arousal levels shot up. After the levels returned to normal the
subjects were told to recall or visualize an experience that made them feel loved or loving. In both
cases the intensity of the physical reactions that were
being monitored—pulse, heart rate, perspiration,
muscle tension—were virtually identical.

What defines the emotion, then, is the label we put
on it (or the one we have learned to give it). Since we

traditionally think of feeling loved as a positive experience, the physiological responses that accompany it—rapid heartbeat, flushed skin, sinking stomach, quick breathing, a surge of energy or a sense of pleasant lassitude—are labeled delightful and gratifying. But because we traditionally think of being criticized as a negative experience, the same set of responses is labeled unpleasant.

By giving arousal symptoms a negative label we thwart the chances of dealing with criticism in a constructive way. When negative emotions get out of hand, energy is wasted. But if you can take charge of your emotions and the labels you assign to them and refuse to let them work against your own best interests, two advantages accrue. First, your appraisal of criticism is less likely to be clouded by "hurt" feelings. Second, emotional energy can be channeled into confronting criticism confidently.

How do you take charge of your emotions?

Focus on the physical sensations themselves rather than on the mental label you may be inclined to give them. Instead of reacting to a suddenly faster heartbeat or a rush of blood to the skin by telling yourself, *I'm angry,* try to isolate the arousal symptoms by identifying them simply as a physiological cue that you may be on the verge of losing emotional control.

If you label the arousal as "anger," you are virtually predetermining your consequent words and actions; for example, you may believe you have a right to argue back, to yell, or to threaten the other person. If you label your arousal symptoms as "anxiety" or "fear," you may short-circuit your capacity for judgment, perhaps retreat from the encounter entirely, or become angry at yourself for giving in to qualms.

By labeling the arousal negatively you are implying to yourself that the situation is already out of control. By recognizing the symptoms of arousal without giving them an emotional label you can make them serve as an "early warning system" —a signal that something is going on in your body, but that you do not intend to let the reactions get out of control.

Positive self-statements can provide the cognitive feedback needed to channel arousal symptoms into a productive course. Tell yourself: *Stay calm. Breathe deeply. Don't clench your fists.* Try to combine these statements with those you use to encourage objective appraisal of criticism. For example: *Stay calm; what this person is saying may be helpful if I listen carefully. Try to relax; nobody is trying to hurt me.*

Use your emotions as a source of energy; make them stimulate rather than devitalize you. Any negative emotion exerts an energy drain. Think of the shakiness, the emptiness, the weakness we feel after being angry or apprehensive. But physiological arousal can be converted into a source of positive energy if we use it to "psych ourselves up." This is a common technique in competitive sports, where athletes often deliberately raise their arousal level to charge their emotional batteries. Football players say that once they make that first run from scrimmage, or that first tackle, their nervousness disappears and is replaced by confidence.

Nervous energy can be used in a similar way to prepare for criticism and defuse its intensity. Psychologist Richard Lazarus, writing in the professional journal *American Psychologist*, makes the point this way:

> Much coping activity is anticipatory; that is, the person expects a future harmful confrontation, such as failing an examination, performing in public . . . or [receiving] a personal criticism, and this leads him to prepare against the future possibility of harm. To the extent that he prepares effectively . . . he thereby changes the nature of the ultimate transaction, along with the *emotions that might have been experienced* [italics ours]. . . . Overcoming the danger before it materializes can lead to exhilaration rather than fear, grief, [or] depression.[5]

Learning to relax physically is a third technique for taking charge of your emotions. When your body is relaxed you are reducing stress and conserving energy—both key factors in keeping arousal levels low. Since it is impossible to feel hurt or angry at the same time that you feel relaxed, you will be able to be more receptive to criticism. There are many excellent relaxation exercises. Here is one that combines several of the most effective techniques.

Find a quiet place where you will not be disturbed for at least fifteen minutes. Sit in a comfortable chair, or lie on a couch, bed, or on the floor. Support your neck with a firm pillow. Loosen tight clothing and remove jewelry and contact lenses. Begin the exercise by heightening muscle tension and then releasing it:

—Make a clenched fist . . . tighten it . . . then release.

—Suck in your stomach muscles until you can imagine that your stomach is touching your back. Hold the position ten seconds, then release.

—Clench your teeth, press your jaws together, hold, then release.

—Close your eyes and squeeze your eyelids firmly together; hold and release.

—Push down on head and neck so they sink between your shoulders. Feel the tension in shoulder and neck muscles, then release.

—Inhale and hold your breath as long as possible. Exhale as if you were trying to force all the air out of a balloon.

—Stretch out arms and legs and hold them stiffly, then release.

—Try combining these exercises until you can do several, if possible, all of them, simultaneously.

—Allow your body to go limp so that a wave of gentle relaxation flows from forehead to feet. Concentrate on smoothing out tension around your eyes, forehead, mouth, neck, and back.

Still sitting or lying in a comfortable position, hold your thumbnail a few inches from your eyes and focus all your attention on it. Feel your hand getting heavier, your eyelids getting heavier, your breathing becoming deeper and slower. Slowly allow your hand to fall to your side and your eyes to close. As you inhale and exhale, count each breath, imagining that you are sinking into an ever-deeper relaxation with each number. At the count of ten indulge in self-guided imagery by visualizing yourself in whatever circumstance you consider pleasant—floating in a pool on a rubber raft, sprawling on thick grass, stretched out in a warm bath, or walking in the woods after a refreshing rain shower. Hold this scene in your mind's eye as long as possible.

Your body and mind are now prepared for the important message you want to give yourself. Though you will want to choose your own words, it goes something like this: *When I am being criticized I will remain as relaxed as I am now. I will use criticism to my best advantage, to help me grow to become the best person that I can be.*

Before bringing yourself out of the relaxed state by slowly counting from ten to one, be aware of how good it feels to gain control over your thoughts, emotions, and actions. Tell yourself that this relaxed awareness and the positive attitude it engenders will persist.

The Need for Action

A positive response to criticism means accepting it both constructively and effectively. Those words are not synonymous. Constructive acceptance involves appraising a criticism accurately to determine if it is valid; keeping lines of communication open between yourself and the criticizer; controlling negative emotions; and, last, recognizing that it may be time to do something about the criticized behavior. Effective acceptance occurs when you do take action to change.

Many of us never reach the point of taking action. We dismiss the criticism as invalid, or disregard it, or argue with the critic, or allow ourselves to be so crushed by the criticism that we can't take positive action. Sometimes it seems that it is too late to change. Even if we accept a criticism constructively we may have trouble implementing it. To say, in effect, "You are right; I am wrong," may be a partially constructive response, but it is certainly not an effective one.

Consider the case of a woman who criticized her husband for the consistently slipshod way he handled transactions in their joint checking account. Having learned how to do this constructively, she did not make a comment such as, "You loused up the checking account again this month! Why do you always forget to enter the amount when you write a check?" Instead she said, "We were charged a five dollar fee again this month because our checking account was overdrawn. I thought we had enough in the account to cover the phone bill I paid, but evidently you neglected to record a check you wrote last week. Next time you write a check, will you remember to make a note to yourself, or to me, so we can keep the balance accurate?"

"I'm sorry about that," the husband replied. "You're absolutely right to criticize me. From now on I'll be more careful."

But the next month the man forgot to enter two checks, and the account again was overdrawn and charged a penalty. The wife once more remonstrated, the husband once more promised to reform, and the following month the same thing happened. Though he accepted his wife's criticism in a superficially constructive way, by making no change in his behavior the man was not accepting it effectively.

To resolve a criticism requires a commitment to action in word and deed. Let's look first at communication techniques you can use to initiate behavior change:

Do not defend yourself against the criticism. All too often the instinctive reaction is to contradict or disavow the charge, or to try to excuse our actions.

> HUSBAND: You left the lights on in the living room all night again. You're just wasting money.
> WIFE: It wasn't my fault, I wasn't the last one to go to bed.

We may retaliate by accusing the other person of similar shortcomings:

> HUSBAND: You left the lights on all night again. You're just wasting money.
> WIFE: Well, I'm not the only one. You waste money too.

Or we may try to divert attention from ourselves by charging the critic with failings of his or her own:

> HUSBAND: You left the lights on all night again. You're just wasting money.
> WIFE: You're not perfect, either. Remember the time you forgot the keys and locked us out of the house?

When you defend yourself against criticism you handicap your chances of dealing with it effectively.

When you could be talking or thinking about how to correct the criticized behavior, you are blurring the issue. Some people are greatly skilled at this sort of game playing, but the result is hardly a victory. Denials and counterattacks merely increase the likelihood of a counterproductive exchange. As you become more skilled in appraising criticism you will find there is less reason to defend yourself.

Ask for more information. Being action oriented means seeking out data, not just accepting whatever is offered. Though one of the hallmarks of giving constructive criticism is being specific, many people fail to do this. Therefore, you must ask for details. If the criticism is vague or generalized, ask for a particular example. Ask *when* the incident occurred, *where* it occurred, *what* was especially annoying about your behavior. (One caution: do *not* ask questions in a brusque or demanding way, as if you were a police officer interrogating a suspect; phrase them to indicate that you want the criticizer's help.)

Obtaining additional information accomplishes four things. It helps you appraise the criticism more accurately. It gives you concrete examples of the behavior for which you are being criticized. It shows that you are concerned about the situation. And it converts a negative interaction into a potentially positive dialogue.

Develop the skill of attentive listening. Research shows that the average person grasps only one-third of what he or she hears, and remembers accurately only half of that third. We can listen nearly five times as fast as we can speak; in the time it takes for a criticizer to say a hundred words, the person being criticized has "brain room" for five hundred words. The excess capacity is usually given over to preparing denials or rebuttals. In addition—and this is particularly true when we are being criticized—we tend to screen out much of what we do not *want* to hear. If criticism is frequent we are likely to tune it out.

Try to keep your own emotions from interfering with your listening efficiency. Sometimes they can turn a noncritical remark into what seems to be a critical one. When one woman told her husband that the new clothing styles left her with "nothing to wear," he flew into a rage. Sensitive about his earning capacity, he heard her as implying that he did not earn enough to support her properly. In another instance a man who mildly complained about his children's table manners was startled when his wife interpreted his remark as a criticism of the way she brought them up.

It is also important for the person *giving* criticism to listen attentively. "My dad had nagged me for weeks to clear away piles of old magazines that were cluttering the attic," a teenager said. "One day I rolled up my sleeves and threw them all out. When I told him about it I thought he would be pleased, but all he said was 'Uh-huh.' A little while later, he suddenly said to me, 'When are you going to get rid of that junk in the attic?' He hadn't heard a word I'd said!"

Ask for solutions to the criticism. Your questions can be as indirect as "What would you do about this if you were in my place?" or as direct as "How can I

do this better?" or "What would you like me to do?"
The more specific your questions the better:

> WIFE TO HUSBAND (after changing her
> hairstyle): How do you think this looks?
> HUSBAND: Terrible. It's all frizzy.
> WIFE: Well, what style do you think
> would look better?

Asking for help has several beneficial results. For
one, you focus discussion on effective action, thereby
creating the important psychological effect (for both
persons) of implying that there is a productive way to
resolve the criticism, and that you are open to it. For
another, you convert the criticism process from a
one-way thrust to a team effort. By asking, in effect,
"How can *we* deal with this?" you are increasing the
commitment of the criticizer to your common goal.
Finally, asking for help taps the creative resources of
the critic. You don't have to generate new approaches single-handedly; and you are not left with
the unsettling sense of not knowing what to do next.

*Summarize what both you and the other person
have said.*   A good listener does not assume he understands what has been said; he makes sure of it
before he responds. Some counselors recommend
that after any complex or heated discussion you repeat back to the other person—in your own words—
what you believe both of you have said. Counseling
psychologist Carl Rogers has called this the "echo
game." This feedback technique can also be used to
make sure both persons agree on realistic goals for
behavior change. Rather than saying, "I'll work on

it," or "I'll try to do better," you can establish parameters for exactly what you will do, how you will do it, and when you will do it.

Strategies for Change

Now, some basic strategies for action you can take to initiate and carry out behavior change.

Make a "contract" with yourself.   Marriage counselors use contracts to encourage couples to act on the insights they develop during counseling. The contract is a mutual agreement, sometimes verbal but usually written, in which partners commit themselves to make new plans, set new goals, or adopt a certain kind of new behavior. You can contract with *yourself* to change behavior if you have assessed a criticism to be valid.

To be effective, a contract cannot be vaguely formulated in your mind. It should be written and spell out exactly what behavior is involved and how you specifically intend to change it. Suppose you have been criticized for smoking too much. The contract should specify:

1.   The exact number of cigarettes you will limit yourself to each twenty-four hours. To say merely "I will not smoke so many cigarettes" is meaningless.

2.   A deadline when the contract will be fulfilled. Set a realistic time limit. Promising yourself to reach the goal in two weeks may be too short a time, but giving yourself six months is too long.

3.   A reward for reaching the goal. You must give yourself this positive reinforcement *as soon as* the

contract is fulfilled. It can be as simple as having a meal in a fine restaurant or buying a book you have wanted to read, or as elaborate as treating yourself to a vacation. But you must carry out this self-promise. (There can even be a "bonus" clause, giving yourself an extra reward if you do better than expected. Conversely, there must be a penalty if you fail to reach your goal. This negative reinforcement must also take place promptly, and it should be as aversive as the incentive is rewarding.)

4. How the changed behavior is to be verified. To determine if a change has actually occurred you may contract to count the number of cigarettes smoked each day, or how much less money you spent on cigarettes per week. There needs to be some genuine evidence that you have fulfilled your basic contract.

Monitor your behavior. As much as possible, observe and record your behavior. Just doing that will help to bring about a change. For instance, in the example above you might keep a list showing when and where you smoked each cigarette. After a while convert the list into a chart or graph so that you can "see" the change that is taking place. This provides positive reinforcement as well.

Break down the behavior to be changed into a series of separate "assignments." A lawyer we know was frequently criticized by his wife for letting their home slide into clutter and disrepair. "There are dozens of things that need to be fixed around here," she would complain. And he would groan, "I'll never have time to do them all."

Obviously it is difficult to begin to take any action

if one sets too arduous or exacting a goal. But if you can break the goal down into a series of separate and manageable tasks—scheduling the easiest one, or the one with the highest probability of success, first— change suddenly appears more feasible. In this in- stance the husband listed everything that needed re- pairs, set a relaxed timetable for the work and approached the tasks one at a time. He spent half a day cleaning out the garage, part of the following weekend weeding and pruning in the garden, twenty minutes one evening repairing a leaky faucet, and so on. Soon it no longer seemed unlikely that every- thing eventually would be taken care of.

Make it harder to continue the criticized behavior by surrounding it with obstacles. Psychologists sometimes call this "narrowing the stimulus." That means using the environment to help you behave differently. Are you criticized for picking too many arguments? Make a rule that you may not argue in any room except, say, the living room, which you are in least often. Are you criticized for watching televi- sion too much and studying too little? Move the set to a seldom-used room; take away the comfortable chair and replace it with one that has no arms and a straight back; if the "vertical hold" slips, don't fix it. Meanwhile, make the area where you study as invit- ing and cozy as possible. As watching television be- comes increasingly troublesome and uncomfortable, it will be easier to adopt the desired new behavior.

We have talked about the constructive use of thoughts, emotions and behavior as if they were quite separate ways of responding to criticism. But it is worth reemphasizing that they are inextricably interwoven, just as they are in giving criticism. Each element interacts with the others. Making thoughts work for you depends on how well you take charge of your emotions, and vice versa. Managing thoughts and emotions may still prove unproductive unless you also recognize the need for action.

No one enjoys taking criticism, but learning how to accept it constructively gives you an important source of personal feedback and a vital tool for personal growth. The fact is that you are going to get—and need—criticism as long as you interact with others, which means as long as you live. It is essential for your own happiness that you learn to use it well.

5 | The Delicate Art of Sexual Criticism

Our sex life isn't nearly as good as it used to be. I still love my husband, but his lovemaking is so predictable that it's become boring. Yet how can I say that to him?

———

I try to please her, but I guess I'm not succeeding. If only she would tell me what she wants.

———

Ever since she told me she's been faking orgasms, that she's never really had one, I haven't been able to touch her. I feel as if I've been castrated.

Of all forms of criticism, sexual criticism is without doubt the most difficult to utter and the most devastating to hear. Nothing can be more stressful or embarrassing than to point out a partner's sexual failings. Nothing can diminish one's self-esteem so sharply as to be told one is an inadequate or unsatisfactory lover. And nothing can scar a relationship so deeply or painfully as derogatory comments about a partner's sexual skills, or even well-meaning suggestions that can be construed as being unkindly critical.

No wonder therapists say that in fully half of all marriages tensions are heightened and conflicts aggravated by destructive words about a partner's sexual performance. But does that mean sexual criticism should be avoided or repressed? Not if we bear in mind the concept of criticism as a tool to enhance growth.

The fact is that most men and women have never learned how to discuss ways of making sex better except by complaining about the way it is. Yet lovemaking is not an instinctual skill; it is an art that must be learned, and positive criticism can be not only a useful teaching aid, but a way of showing one's appreciation for a partner's efforts to be a better sexual companion.

Indeed, it is virtually impossible to improve a sexual relationship unless the two persons involved are able to share and exchange potentially helpful information—in other words, to be constructively critical. "Sex usually must be directly confronted before it can be changed," sociologist John Gagnon observed. But if such a confrontation can contribute to a more rewarding sex life for both partners, why do most of us find it so uncomfortable to initiate, and so distressing to accept?

There are several reasons. For one thing, frank talk of any kind about sex is still a schizophrenic issue. On the one hand we take for granted the near-constant bombardment of sexual incidents, allusions and descriptions which routinely appear in books, movies, television, and advertising. Yet at the same time we hesitate to voice our *personal* sexual feelings. Since earliest childhood most people have been taught that it is "wrong" to mention them openly. As a result, they are blocked from talking about sexual needs, desires and disappointments.

Second, we have learned to tread carefully in this criticism minefield lest sexual egos be trampled. Criticism that implies (or can be inferred to mean) that one is not a good lover strikes at the most fragile and sensitive component of self-esteem. We seldom stop to think how strange this is. No one automatically assumes that he or she, without schooling and experience, could be a competent artist, craftsman, scientist or chef. Nor is anyone born with a special talent for lovemaking. And not since the days of the professional courtesans has anyone been trained for it. Yet almost every person likes to believe he or she is—or should be—a competent lover.

Since we know how *we* would feel if someone criticized our sexual technique, we hesitate to criticize a partner's for fear of inflicting the same kind of hurt. "How can I tell my wife she doesn't satisfy me in bed?" a man asks. "It would destroy her." He does not realize he has probably already conveyed that message in a dozen different ways *without* words. But by not bringing the criticism out into the open so that something can be done to remedy the problem, he is consigning his wife to a lingering sense of puzzlement, guilt or anger even while she does not know exactly what may be wrong.

Sexual criticism—unlike some other kinds—thus inevitably affects both giver and receiver. One woman who complained about her partner's insensitivity to her needs felt guilty, later, about what she had said: "I'm only criticizing him for my own benefit. Is it fair to hurt his feelings just so I can get more out of our lovemaking?"

In other instances sexual criticism may be inhibited because one partner feels the problem is his or her own fault and has nothing to do with the other person: "What's the use of complaining that I can't reach a climax when I'm the one to blame?" a woman said.

Still another barrier to sexual criticism is the fact that we lack a proper language for it. Literally, as well as figuratively, we are at a loss for the proper words. Despite the liberalization of language, most people are still uncomfortable with blunt or vulgar sexual terminology; yet the scientific terms for sexual activities and organs sound too clinical. So to talk about intimate relationships in terms of "coitus" or "fellatio" can be just as disconcerting or embarrassing as to discuss them in more vulgar, popular terms. Perhaps that is one reason why, as we shall see, much sexual criticism is conveyed, consciously or unconsciously, by gesture, voice tone, muscle tension, body movement, and degrees of touching.

Criticizing a Sexual Partner

A good deal of sexual criticism stems from circumstances that have little or nothing to do with the partner one is criticizing. For example, Ray believed that he was being sexually shortchanged because his wife was not overtly passionate during lovemaking. Ray had read enough erotic novels to "know" how a truly aroused woman behaved: she breathed faster, moaned and gasped; her body arched and writhed; her fingernails dug into her partner's skin. But when Ray and his wife made love she did none of these things. Instead, her response was gentle—not because she was unexcited, but because that was the inherent nature of her reaction. Ray began to feel cheated, deprived of the rewards his unrealistic view of sex told him he was supposed to have. He also felt put down, thinking that it must be *his* inadequacy that left his wife so unstirred. Unable, finally, to control his frustration and disappointment, Ray angrily criticized his wife for her passivity: "You never move your body. You hardly ever make a sound! What's wrong with you?"

Like Ray, many men and women have vastly unrealistic expectations about sex, both for their own performances and for a partner's response. Fantasizing about sex—creating scenarios that are erotically arousing or perhaps imagining that one is making love with a movie star is one thing. So long as fantasy does not substitute for reality, and so long as it does not produce guilt, it can enhance sexual experience. But some people measure their own (or a partner's) skills by fantasized ideals. They believe that everyone else is enjoying ecstatic sex every night; they imagine every woman capable of having multiple orgasms, and every man capable of endlessly sustained intercourse. Such fantasies are likely to end in inappropriate criticism based on a distorted view of what fulfilling sex should be like.

Inappropriate criticism also stems from expectations that are not so much unrealistic as unspoken. Psychiatrist Clifford Sager has pointed out that each of us enters a relationship carrying a bundle of expectations and promises, both conscious and unconscious, expressed and unexpressed. The unconscious and unexpressed expectations and promises form a "secret agenda" —an emotional contract one partner is making with another, but a contract that neither is aware exists. Such contracts can cover every conceivable aspect of a relationship: power, children, money, leisure-time activities, and sex.[6]

For example, 27-year-old Amy and 36-year-old Martin edged to the brink of divorce when his repeated criticism of her for not being sufficiently interested in sex grew too hostile for Amy to handle. She also thought the criticism was undeserved. When the therapist they consulted took the couple's sexual history, Amy pointed out that she and Martin made love an average of twice a week.

"The only times I decline," she said, "are when I'm really exhausted from my job, or when I don't feel well." Martin admitted that the facts Amy stated were correct—yet still he accused her of "rejecting" him sexually. After several counseling sessions the therapist was able to uncover the "contract" Martin had unwittingly taken with him into his marriage with Amy—an emotional bargain of which she was completely unaware.

"Martin was essentially an insecure person," the

therapist said. "His father had died when he was only eight years old, and his mother, who had always been emotionally constricted, became even more so. In her mind, her husband's death had 'proved' that giving and getting affection was too dangerous a risk to take. So Martin grew up in a cold, correct, but essentially loveless atmosphere. As a result, what he unconsciously wanted most from a relationship with a woman was total emotional acceptance—which to him was signified by constantly available sex. Martin's contract ran something like this: 'I will be a good husband, and take care of you and any children we may have, but in return you are to give me warm sex whenever I want it.'

"But this had never been spelled out to Amy," the therapist continued. "She had no conception of Martin's need, and no idea of the unspoken contract he expected her to honor. As a result she saw his complaint at first as an exploitative demand, and then as undeserved criticism."

Basing sexual expectations on arbitrary or external standards is another cause of inappropriate criticism. One woman's husband accused her of being undersexed because they made love only once a week, whereas he had read that the "average" couple in their age bracket had sex three times a week. Therapists are constantly being asked by couples how often they "should" have intercourse, how long foreplay "should" last, whether oral sex is "normal." But there are no rules—no "shoulds and shouldn'ts," no "rights and wrongs" —for sex between consenting adults. Nor should anyone be judged by comparison to others. Some couples may happily have sex twice a day; others may be just as happy making love twice a month, or even twice a year. Criticizing a partner because he or she fails to measure up to some mythical average or arbitrary norm is a foolish mistake.

Sexual criticism is also misplaced when it stems from inaccurate information about human sexuality. Most women today know that the capacity for orgasm varies widely from person to person, and that there is more than one way to reach a climax. But a woman who is not aware of these facts, and who rarely experiences orgasm, may berate herself with destructive criticism: *There must be something wrong with me.* If her partner is equally ill-informed, he may reproach himself for not being able to bring her to orgasm. Similarly an older man, who does not know that the refractory period (the length of time after ejaculation before a man can have another erection) increases with age, may blame himself for being unable to perform as often as he once could. If his partner is also ignorant of this normal physiological change, she may belittle him for a "lack" of masculinity.

The greater danger, of course, is that sexual criticism can become a self-fulfilling prophecy. A man or woman repeatedly criticized for fancied sexual failings may actually develop a sexual dysfunction. The most important sexual organ, experts remind us, is the mind. If we allow ourselves to become psychologically convinced—through criticism or other means—that we are somehow sexually inadequate, that inadequacy may become physiologically real.

Impotence, for example, is frequently the result of a man's fear that he will not be potent.

Sex, as Masters and Johnson point out, is perhaps the ultimate form of male-female communication. Thus bedroom criticism often extends quickly to other phases of a relationship. But the converse is also true. The sexual relationship can become the mirror for the whole relationship, and criticisms and conflicts in nonsexual areas may be displaced onto the sexual. As a result, hurtful remarks about a partner's sexual abilities may have nothing to do with sex at all. They may be voiced as a way of getting revenge, or of establishing dominance, or of creating a sense of inferiority in a partner so the other can control him or her. A passive person, unable to make demands in other areas of a relationship, may use sexual criticism as a way of releasing repressed anger or hostility.

The effects of destructive sexual criticism need not be belabored. It not only spoils sex at the moment, but also leaves a bitter aftertaste. In some men and women it arouses concerns which may lessen their interest in, or response to, future sexual encounters. Instead of experiencing sensations, they are distracted by self-conscious thoughts: *Am I going too fast? Too slow? Is my touch too gentle or too rough? Am I pleasing my partner or not?*

When criticism kindles such anxieties, one becomes more a spectator than a participant, and a self-critical spectator at that. The focus of lovemaking then shifts to performance rather than pleasure. Yet the paradox of sex is that if it is pleasurable, one can be reasonably certain that whatever one is doing is being done well.

Criticism-induced anxiety over performance can result in impotence, an inability to reach orgasm, premature ejaculation, and other sexual dysfunctions. Conversely, if negative criticism is withheld even such dysfunctions (if they are indeed psychological in origin) can be overcome by the gradual growth of intimacy.

Psychiatrist Raymond Babineau, writing in the professional journal, *Medical Aspects of Human Sexuality*, describes a couple who were both virgins at marriage.

> [At first] the husband tended to ejaculate fairly rapidly and the wife seldom was orgasmic during intercourse. . . . Fortunately, neither of them thought of the situation as dysfunctional and saw encouraging signs of slow improvement as the months went by. . . . After eight years of marriage . . . they felt well-adjusted sexually to one another. The husband had been aided by the passage of time and had less urgent ejaculatory need. The wife was quite confident now of her orgasmic capacity and . . . felt more interested in sex than eight years previously.
>
> This couple had the good fortune to grow together sexually. We can guess what might have happened if they had been more critical of their partners. She might have said, "You are a selfish premature ejaculator." He might have said, "You have a hang-up about orgasms." Alternatively, they might have been intensely self-critical: "Something must be terribly wrong with me."[7]

All the customary tactics of destructive criticism discussed in earlier chapters are too often used in criticizing a sexual partner. For example:

GENERALIZATION: You *never* spend enough time in foreplay. Or, you *always* take too long to reach a climax.

FAULTY FEEDBACK: I wish you wouldn't touch me that way. [*What* way?]

SHAMING: What's happened to you? There isn't much starch in that erection.

BLAMING: If you could last longer I wouldn't feel so frustrated.

ACCUSING QUESTION: Is that what you call being gentle?

But sexual criticism can also be communicated in a number of other, more subtle and even more damaging ways. Tactile criticism, for instance, can wordlessly convey sexual uninterest or displeasure: moving away from a proffered embrace, or remaining rigid and unyielding within one; pushing away a partner's hand; keeping one's lips pressed tightly together while being kissed; or turning one's face away from a kiss entirely. A man who suddenly loses his erection, or a woman who fails to lubricate, may be saying with their bodies that their partners are failing to excite them.

Nor is negative criticism limited to the act of love-making itself. Some people pick arguments, provoke anxieties or make demands immediately before or after sex. Creating tension and stress effectively destroys sensual feelings. So does insisting on certain kinds of sexual positions or sexual play.

Destructive sexual criticism often sets up a fear of rejection or abandonment that can lead to a self-defeating "criticism loop." "It's reached the point where I'm terrified every time we make love," a woman says. "All I can think is, what if I don't please him, what if I don't have an orgasm? I don't want to lose him, but I know he's finding fault with me just so he'll have an excuse to leave me."

Other sexual partners may react to the implicit threat in criticism with defensive hostility. "Every time she gets on me for something I'm supposed to be doing wrong in bed, I tell her what *she's* doing wrong," one husband said. In this kind of vicious circle the content of the criticism becomes meaningless. "I don't think either of us pays any attention to what's being said," the man continued. "We're too busy defending ourselves by counterattacking."

But lovers must be able to trust each other if sex between them is going to be good. Dr. Helen Kaplan, one of America's foremost sex therapists, believes that mutual trust is one of the psychological essentials for reaching orgasm. Yet it is impossible to feel trusting and secure with a partner who habitually criticizes in a negative manner. It is important, therefore, for partners to know how to offer sexual criticism in a positive way, and also how to accept it constructively.

How to Give Sexual Criticism

Before saying anything to your partner that is of a critical nature, ask yourself these key questions: *What is the reason for my criticism?* Unless there is a good, constructive reason, say nothing. *Is this the optimum place or moment to be critical?* If not, ask yourself, *When and where can I best communicate this information so that it will enhance our sexual relationship?*

When you do offer criticism, remember to emphasize the pleasure your partner gives you rather than concentrate on what he or she does that you dislike. Instead of saying, "I don't enjoy it when you fondle me so roughly," say, "I really love it when you touch me gently." When you communicate a dislike, rather than a preference, you are forcing your partner (and yourself) to focus on details of sexual performance rather than on sexual feelings and expressions.

Be careful, when communicating your preferences, that you do not make your words sound like a command. When you issue an order such as, "Touch me gently," the implication is, "or else I won't let you touch me at all." Similarly, preferences should not be voiced in the context of a threat: "If you don't know how to make love to me the way I like to be loved, I will find somebody who does."

Try not to criticize a sexual partner for something he or she cannot change. Criticizing a partner's physical attributes—such as size of penis or shape of breasts—is maliciously cruel; nothing short of cosmetic surgery can alter most such conditions. Criticizing a partner's sexual appetite or capacity is also bound to be counterproductive.

As we have noted, the sexual hyperbole portrayed in books and films has led many men and women to expect a partner to perform heroic sexual feats. But in real life only the rare individual can make love for hours with unflagging energy. In real life most people are reluctant to experiment with extravagant sexual techniques. Criticizing someone for being unable to fulfill your unrealistic expectations (or even your realistic ones) can only serve to make him or her more tense, more angry, and less loving.

Phrase your criticism in terms of "I" rather than "you" —in terms of desires rather than recriminations. For example, "Your whiskers are scratching me! Why don't you shave before we make love?" will be more effective in changing behavior when it becomes, "I really like the way your skin feels when it is smooth." A criticism such as "Why do you insist on making love with the lights out?" will get a more positive response if it is rephrased, "I love to see your body and face when we make love."

Avoid abstract criticisms. "I've seen many clients lately who tell me their partners blame them because sex is boring," a therapist says. "But what does that mean? 'Boring' can characterize a dozen different sexual lacks. Is the setting unimaginative? The timing wrong? The sex play perfunctory? The whole thing too repetitive? And what is the criticized partner supposed to do about it? To be useful, a criticism must be concrete and specific."

Use the "rephrasing" technique to convert negative sounding comments to positive ones. There is a vast difference between complaining about what you do not get out of sex, on the one hand, and on the other proposing what it is you would like to experience and then discussing how that might be accomplished. After all, can you reasonably expect a partner to listen sympathetically when you point out how he or she does *not* please you? Try focusing on what he or she *does* do to please you—and then offer constructive suggestions as to how your lovemaking can be made even better.

Avoid comparisons. Perhaps the most deadly form of criticism is that which compares a current partner's sexual skills with those of a previous partner.

Take some responsibility yourself for making sex more rewarding or exciting instead of expecting a partner to do it single-handedly. "I know there are times when I need extra stimulation," one woman said, "so I take some of the responsibility for doing something about it. Perhaps I'll put on an especially provocative negligee. Perhaps I'll encourage my erotic feelings by fantasizing a sexual scene, or reading an arousing novel. The point is that *I* try to create an emotional atmosphere in which change can take place."

Similarly, helping a partner who is trying to meet your criticism is more effective than acting like a judgmental observer. For instance, one man frequently criticized his wife for her unwillingness to try different sexual positions. His fault finding merely reinforced her attitude. Finally he said, "Look, it's all right to do whatever you want" —at which point she was able to relax and experiment. Giving "permission" for sexual pleasuring is often more effective in dissolving inhibitions than haranguing a partner about them. In the long run any positive change in sexual behavior depends on the mutual involvement of *both* partners.

Criticize through demonstration. When words would be abrasive, or when it would be difficult to put one's desires into specific form, *showing* is more effective than telling a partner what you would like him or her to do. A woman who was particularly aroused by breast caresses complained to a sex therapist that her husband rarely touched her there. "And how do you handle the situation?" the therapist inquired.

"I wait for him to make the first move," she replied. "When he doesn't, I feel rejected—I begin to think that my breasts are too small, or that there is something about them that repels him. I want to ask him, but I can't bring myself to do that because I'm afraid to hear what he might say."

"Next time you are making love," the therapist suggested, "don't wait for him. You take the initiative. Take his hand and place it on your breast. Move his hand the way you would want him to move it. Tell him that you like the way that feels. By demonstrating what you want your husband to do—and by showing how you respond to his touch—you will be more likely to change his pattern of love play." Words, especially when they are heard as demands, tend to perpetuate rigid sexual attitudes. Actions, when performed lovingly, tend to increase a partner's sensory awareness and help to initiate new sexual behavior.

How to Accept Sexual Criticism

When you are criticized by a sexual partner, keep your own reactions under control. Use reason to appraise the validity of the criticism, to make sure you understand it, and to assess its emotional overtones.

Ask what your partner meant by his or her words or actions. Never assume that you know. If necessary, repeat back to your partner what you understood the criticism to imply. Paraphrase the criticism before jumping to conclusions about its meaning.

Challenge your partner to search for the underlying significance of his or her criticism with such statements as, "Tell me more about that," or "Can you expand on what you are saying?" or "I'd like to know how that makes you feel." If the criticism was a general statement— "Sex is getting boring" —ask for specific complaints or suggestions for change.

Suggest to a partner that he or she discuss sexual needs and wants in specific as well as general terms: "You aren't affectionate after we've made love. I would like you to pay more attention to me after sex. I wish you would hold me for a while afterwards."

To accept sexual criticism constructively, you need to know your partner's motives for expressing it. No matter how hurt or defensive you may feel at the moment, it is important to find out, insofar as possible, *why* the criticism was uttered. Again, you have to ask questions.

— "Did you say that to make me feel bad? Or because you felt bad?"

— "Was your criticism a reaction to something I said or did that made you feel hurt, put down or attacked?"

— "Is this something you've been keeping to yourself a long time? If so, why did you let it out now? What happened just now to make you say that?"

— "Do you think that what you are criticizing is truly under my control, something I can change? If so, can you tell me how?"

Make every effort to get the criticizer to probe beneath his or her conscious reasons to the unconscious motives.

Perhaps the most significant factor in the constructive acceptance of criticism is trust—the committed belief that even though a partner's words may be thoughtless or even cruel, he or she is honestly trying to preserve or improve the relationship.

In many cases trust is undermined because partners are unaware of the emotional effect sexual criticism can have. In a counseling session, for example, a therapist asked a woman how her husband's disapproving comment made her feel. "I felt angry and humiliated," she said.

"But that is a label, not a feeling," the therapist

pointed out. "What were your emotional reactions?"

"Well," the woman replied, "I guess I started to cry, and I felt as if I couldn't breathe."

The therapist turned toward the woman's husband. "Did you mean to make her feel that way?"

"Heavens no," came the prompt answer. "I didn't want to hurt her. I *love* her!"

Without mutual understanding and trust a cycle of criticism can lead to negative sexual conditioning. Another therapist describes the case of a couple whose previously joyous sex life sputtered to a halt because both partners reacted badly to real or fancied criticism:

"Each time one of them felt wounded, he or she sought revenge by rebuffing the other's next sexual advance. As time went on the couple's once-wide range of sexual expression became restricted and constrained. Instead of talking out their resentments, each partner acted them out by avoiding the sexual contact in which each had originally been hurt."

The Mask of "Honesty"

A word needs to be said about sexual criticism that masquerades under the guise of "honesty." Total sexual frankness is something partners volunteer or insist upon at their own not inconsiderable risk. While it is true that good sex depends upon open communication, there are times when too much communication may be more harmful than helpful.

"The problem," writes psychologist Carol Tavris, "is to know not only whether to be candid, but also when and how.... There is a fine difference between not being honest and being dishonest. To restrain an impulse to blurt out a damaging truth is not the same as lying. And the self-satisfied determination to be honest at all costs often can be very costly."[8]

"Honest" criticism often masks ignoble intentions. For example, a woman asks her husband if sex was good for him. Even if it wasn't, under ordinary circumstances he might either say "yes," or avoid the question altogether. Now, however, he is angry about something else, something totally apart from sex. He takes advantage of his "right" to be honest by saying, "Not very . . . but then it seldom is. You're not a very good lover."

Or consider the woman who occasionally does not reach a climax. To a concerned partner she might say, "That was very pleasant. I enjoy making love with you." That would be truer to the higher bond between the couple than saying, "I didn't have an orgasm that time." In another definition, true frankness is not *having* to tell a hurtful truth, but *choosing* to tell it when you believe it would help more than hurt.

The problem for each of us is to know—or at least to sense—when critical frankness might wound rather than help. Constructive honesty, says Tavris, lets a partner know in a loving way what he or she can do to please; destructive honesty says merely that one's partner has failed. It is important, then, to see through the camouflage of "honesty" before you voice a criticism. Ask yourself, *Why am I saying this? What is the purpose of my words? Why am I being more "honest" about sex than I usually am about other things?*

In the last analysis, couples who are able to tell each other their most intimate sexual needs and feelings—whether or not this involves criticisms—report that they have the most rewarding relationships. "Trying to be an effective lover for oneself and one's partner without communicating," says sex therapist Helen Kaplan, "is like trying to learn target shooting blindfolded." With communication, sex moves to a higher level—a level aptly described by writer Brigid Brophy in her novel, *Flesh*:

> Marcus had always imagined that when he did at last make love to a woman it would be in terrible silence, interrupted only by such noises as their bodies might involuntarily make.... But Nancy talked to him about what he was to do, about what he was doing, in a low, rather deep, swift voice which provoked in his skin almost the same sensation as her hands. When he entered her body, he felt he was following her voice.

6 | Children: How to Criticize with Care

Are you going to sleep all day? . . . Who said you could use my hair spray? . . . Clean the dishes off the table. . . . Turn down that radio. . . . Have you made your bed? . . . That skirt is too short. . . . Your closet is a mess. . . . Stand up straight. . . . Somebody has to go to the store. . . . Quit chewing your gum like that. . . . Your hair is too bushy. . . . I don't care if everybody else does have one. . . . Turn down that radio. . . . Have you done your homework? . . . Don't slouch. . . . You didn't make your bed. . . . Quit banging on the piano. . . . Why don't you iron it yourself? . . . Your fingernails are too long. . . . Look it up in the dictionary. . . . Sit up straight. . . . Get off that phone. . . . Why did you ever buy that record? . . . Take the dog out. . . . You forgot to dust that table. . . . You've been in the bathroom long enough. . . . Turn off that radio and go to sleep.

That litany of a day's parental criticisms, entitled "Saturday with a Teenage Daughter," was discovered in a Rhode Island church periodical by child psychologist Dr. Charles Schaefer and quoted in his book, *How to Influence Children.* It was published, presumably, to make parents aware of the extent to which they nag, belittle, bully, badger, and harass their youngsters in the normal course of an ordinary day. Though the description may seem to be exaggerated, chances are that any parent with the stamina to record the number of times he or she criticizes a child in any given day would find it is not that much out of line.

The harsh truth is that most parents incessantly criticize their children in destructive and ineffective ways. Worse yet, the criticism becomes so habitual that many parents are virtually unaware of what they are doing. Some years ago family therapist Dr. Honor Whitney, an authority on the effect of criticism on personality, asked a group of college students to reminisce about their childhoods. One man said he would never forget a phrase his parents had used repeatedly when they were angry with him: *How many times do I have to tell you. . . ?* "It made me feel like a total failure," he said.

"Suddenly everyone was recalling their parents' favorite sayings—and almost all were put-downs," says Dr. Whitney. Not far behind the oft-used "How many times . . . ?" were such disparagements as:
— "Do you expect me to believe *that?*"
— "Look at you . . . you're a mess!"
— "When are you going to grow up?"
— "Can't you do *anything* right?"
— "Now if *that* wasn't a stupid thing to do!"

— "I guess I just can't trust you."

— "You're a bad boy (girl)."

Most of these critical remarks were voiced by mothers. "I will always remember how my mother got after me for every little mistake," a woman said. "She'd be screaming at me and the phone would ring; then she would change the tone of her voice and be charming. . . . I wondered why she treated strangers more politely than her own daughter." Some men and women recalled criticisms that were "impossible" to deal with, such as "Why can't you be more like your brother?" One man said he never understood what his mother meant by such remarks. "What was I supposed to do about it? How was I supposed to feel?"[9]

Children never forget such criticisms. Experiments have proven that every experience is permanently filed for recall in the brain's memory bank. Unfortunately, research indicates that most memory banks are crammed with a collection of parental statements seemingly made with the single aim of belittling or rejecting children.

What makes parents say such terrible things to those they love? Some parents criticize children for behavior they think reflects poorly on themselves. If a youngster is not well behaved—especially in a public place—parents are likely to believe it is their fault (and to assume that others also will believe that). Other parents maintain that criticism is for a child's own good, so that he or she will grow up to be well mannered, obedient, well liked, successful. One such couple, who freely admit to criticizing their

twelve-year-old son "all the time," explain their reasons this way:

> *Mike is a bright boy, but lately he's been doing*
> *poorly in school. When we hear other parents*
> *tell us how well their children are doing, we be-*
> *lieve we have a responsibility for getting Mike to*
> *work harder, to set him straight. So we give him*
> *a little helpful criticism. "You've got to start pay-*
> *ing attention," we told him. "All your friends are*
> *doing better than you are. You don't want to be*
> *the dummy in the group, do you?" Mike always*
> *says he'll try, but nothing happens. We're afraid*
> *he will always have school problems if we don't*
> *keep after him.*

By now the reader can clearly perceive the destructive elements in this criticism. For example, the
lack of specificity (Is Mike doing poorly in everything, or just falling behind in one subject?), the
name calling ("dummy"), and the self-fulfilling
prophecy of the last sentence, to name just a few.

The Long-Term Effects

What are the most common long-term, cumulative
effects that a barrage of destructive criticism can
have on children?

A tendency to avoid or escape the criticizing per-
son, as well as the type of situation or environment in
which the criticism occurred. A parent who frequently ridicules a youngster for being afraid to learn

to swim may instill in the child a permanent aversion to swimming, to deep water, and even, by extension, to beach or lakeshore surroundings. A teacher who harshly criticizes a youngster's work in math class may cause him or her to hate not only math but, again by extension, ultimately all schoolwork and all teachers.

Few children have the inner strength to fight back, or even to protest. A child, wrote George Orwell, "has not accumulated experience to give it confidence in its own judgments. . . . It will accept what it is told, and it will believe in the most fantastic way in the knowledge and power of the adults surrounding it."

The child who receives a great deal of destructive criticism tends to acquire the habit of being destructively critical of others. One of the most powerful ways children learn is by what psychologists call "modeling." If a powerful or important person in a child's life acts or speaks in a certain way, the child will very likely integrate that behavior into his or her own personality and learn to criticize others in a similar way. In criticism workshops we often ask adults, "What effect do you think being criticized as a child had on you?" One woman replied:

> *I'm sure I wasn't aware of the connection then, but my feelings were so hurt that I always wanted to get back at my parents. I'd deliberately misbehave, or say mean things to them. And I criticized my brothers and their friends unmercifully. I guess I'd learned not only how to do it, but that it was okay to do it.*

Unfortunately, the more a child "practices" this learned behavior, and uses it in interpersonal relationships, the more likely he or she is to carry it over into adult life. "When I criticize my daughter," a young father said ruefully, "I remember how my parents were always condemning me for something. I hated it, but now I'm doing the same to my child. If I'm not careful, she's going to grow up and follow my example."

Destructive criticism can sometimes lead to a habit pattern of negative emotional responses—tears, anger, anxiety, resentment. Children may, and justifiably so, interpret criticism as simply another form of punishment. Such negative feelings block productive behavior:

> *When I first tried to teach my seven-year-old son to field ground balls, he kept stepping back or to the side for fear the ball would bounce up and hit him in the face. It made me mad, and I called him a sissy. Then he started to cry and walked away. He wouldn't even play catch with me for weeks afterwards. Eventually we tried it again, and this time I encouraged him when he did well and kept my mouth shut when he shied away. Once he realized I wasn't going to yell at him for mistakes, he learned fast.*

Continued destructive criticism of children too often creates emotional disruption in the entire family. Because criticism is almost always ineffective in changing a youngster's attitudes or behavior, parents eventually tend to blame each other for the lack of results. And blaming becomes a prelude to tensions that are often generalized into other aspects of the husband-wife relationship.

The child also suffers. As the atmosphere of the home is infected with discord, frustrated parents often begin criticizing the child even more for a host of other real or imagined infractions. This "negative halo" effect widens still further the emotional distance between parents and child. The latter can no longer feel sure of the unconditional acceptance and unconditional love that is every youngster's birthright. He or she will make desperate and most often unsuccessful efforts to win parental approval. *To be loved, a child may unconsciously reason, I must heed the criticisms. But since nothing I do is right, and the criticisms continue, obviously I am not capable of being loved.*

A child is less likely to try new behaviors for fear of being criticized by those people who are important to him. A six-year-old rounded the corners of the paper on which she had crayoned a drawing because she thought this made it look prettier. When her kindergarten teacher saw it, she frowned and said, "Now look what you've done! You've ruined it!" From then on the youngster assumed she had no talent at all, and was afraid to try her hand at another drawing.

Conversely, excessive compliments can have the same result. One youngster was so praised for her sketch of a horse that she never drew any other subject, lest she be criticized for not doing it as well.

Destructive criticism damages the self-esteem of

both child and parent.   The parent who constantly criticizes sees himself or herself as ineffective at best, as a "bad parent" at worst. The distressing image may last for years. "My son is twenty-five years old," a man says slowly, "yet I still vividly remember walloping him unmercifully when he was six because he wouldn't stop taking his baby brother's toys. How could I have been such an unfeeling father?"

A child who is consistently and destructively criticized grows up with a sense of bafflement, of vague sorrow, of experiencing his or her world as one of repeated failure. The criticized infant, said the famed psychotherapist Harry Stack Sullivan, develops a generalized feeling of "bad-me." The preschooler with destructively critical parents may become what Sullivan called the "malevolent child" —one who tends to protect his self-image by seeking out and finding only the negative aspects in other people, even if they are gentle and helpful.

Spouse Consensus

There are, as we shall see, a number of specific techniques that help to heighten the effectiveness of criticisms aimed at children. Underlying all of them, however, is a most important general factor: spouse consensus. The phrase refers to the extent to which both parents can agree that the behavior being criticized is actually occurring.

My husband, Ron, is crazy about our little girl. He loves to buy her all sorts of toys. But it upsets him when he comes home from work and finds them all over the living-room floor, the kitchen floor, wherever Carrie has been playing with them. Almost every night he takes Carrie to task for being "sloppy," as he puts it. The other night he actually yelled at her, "Don't be such a sloppy child!"

Of course Ron is a very neat and organized person. But so is Carrie, in her own way. She keeps her room tidy, the teachers say she is neat in her schoolwork, and her friends' mothers always comment on what an orderly child she is. Ron thinks Carrie is sloppy just because she hasn't gotten around to putting her toys away by the time he gets home. But she always does put them away when she's finished playing.

I don't really agree with Ron about criticizing her so much. Every time he calls Carrie "sloppy" I feel bad, she feels unjustly accused, and Ron gets angry.

One goal (and one result) of spouse consensus is that both parents reach and share a common definition of the behavior under criticism. In Carrie's case there was no such consensus. To Ron, "sloppiness" was defined as leaving a few toys scattered about the house. But is that the single or main determinant of "sloppiness"? Not to Ron's wife, it isn't. She knew Carrie would put the toys away in good time; she knew Carrie was extremely neat in other areas of her daily life. With no mutual definition of "sloppiness," Ron's criticism lacked validity—something that Carrie's reaction to it showed she clearly sensed.

Moreover, Ron made no effort to check with his wife before leveling criticism at his daughter. If he had, her greater amount of contact with Carrie during the day would have given him a larger "sample" of the child's behavior on which to make a more reliable judgment. As it was, Ron's perception of Carrie as "sloppy" was based on a single bit of behavior observed at a particular time.

These two principles of spouse consensus—agreement on a definition of the criticized behavior, and accurate mutual observation of whether it occurs a significant amount of the time—help make criticism effective in a number of ways. First, consensus increases the likelihood that the criticism is valid. And since a young child is not able to appraise criticism accurately, consensus performs that function *for* him or her by blocking unfair or invalid criticism.

Second, the process of reaching consensus often alerts the noncritical parent to the fact that some behavior is going on that *needs* to be criticized. It also increases communication between parents and gets both of them actively involved in the situation. (This prevents those "Why didn't you tell me Johnny was bullying other kids?" discussions.)

Third, consensus provides youngsters with a consistent emotional climate in the form of congruent rather than contradictory messages. When children get conflicting criticisms from parents (or criticism from one parent for behavior that is ignored by the other), they are often confused as to what to do. Sometimes they resolve the dilemma by ignoring the criticism—*If I don't hear it I don't have to deal with it.* This may restore the congruence, but it does so in a nonproductive way.

If spouse consensus is not always feasible—as in the case of a single-parent family—the parent can seek corroboration for criticism from relatives, friends or teachers who are with the child for substantial periods of time.

In a school setting, teacher consensus is analogous to spouse consensus. It is important for teachers to share their criticism of a youngster with other teachers who also have that youngster in their classrooms:

> *"Joel was a troublemaker," one physical education teacher said. "I often had to punish the whole gym class by stopping a race or a basketball game because of Joel's actions. But when I talked to teachers who had Joel in their classes, I was surprised to learn they considered him a model pupil.*
>
> *"So I looked more closely at what went on in gym, and I realized Joel's antics were his way of getting back at classmates who teased him because he wasn't good at games or races or exercises. Instead of criticizing Joel as a troublemaker, I tried to help him learn how to deal in a more mature way with the kids who provoked him."*

Criticizing Children

"How can I say anything mean to my child?" a woman asks. "After all, I'm her mother." A father says, "When I criticize my son I feel I'm not doing my job as a parent. I should be helping him, not hurting him." Comments like these are not unusual. They testify to the fact that the false perception of criticism as automatically harmful rather than potentially helpful exerts great influence on parents.

There are other reasons why we hesitate to criticize our children. We may feel that if a youngster is doing something wrong it is our fault for not raising him properly. We identify too much with our children; if they are behaving badly, we think perhaps they learned that behavior from our example. And some parents are afraid to criticize because "If I nag them too much, they won't like me."

According to the late Haim Ginott, an authority on parent-child relationships, most communication between the generations is in the form of two monologues, passing each other unheeded like ships in the night. One, judgmental and fault finding, consists of orders and destructive criticisms; the other consists of fruitless pleadings and denials. The tragedy, Ginott observed, is not that parents lack love or intelligence, but that they lack the skill to communicate with their children effectively.

According to Dr. Charles Schaefer, criticism of children is "most effective when it is task-focused rather than approval-focused." The latter attacks or belittles the person rather than the behavior: "I don't like children who interrupt," or "Only a bad boy keeps interrupting." Task-focused criticism is directed toward the behavior: "I'd appreciate it if you would not interrupt," or "It isn't polite to interrupt when others are speaking."[10]

The aim of this chapter is to provide specific guidelines and techniques for giving effective, task-focused criticism to children. Each shows how to communicate critical information in such a way that a youngster can accept and benefit by it. Each provides a way to give criticism that can promote awareness, growth, change, and self-esteem. Although the techniques use varying approaches, the following guidelines are basic to all of them.

GUIDELINES FOR CRITICIZING CHILDREN:

1. Use words the child can understand.
2. Be sure your criticism is age-appropriate. Don't criticize a youngster for doing (or not doing) something beyond his capabilities.
3. Be brief. Avoid lectures and "preaching."
4. Protect the child's self-image.
5. Be honest.
6. Don't use threats.
7. Be involved. Commit your time and energy to the criticism process. Follow through by helping a youngster deal with the criticism, and praise him or her for responding to it in a positive way.

Strategic Modeling

One of the most consistent findings of psychological research is that children learn by observing other people—especially such important figures as parents, older siblings and teachers. These "significant others," as psychologists call them, in effect serve as models for youngsters' behavior.

The philosopher Joseph Joubert once said that

"Children need models more than they need critics."
But a model can be a critic, and a most effective one
at that. We have already seen—in the example of
youngsters with destructively critical parents who
learn to behave that way themselves—how modeling
can work in a negative way. Similarly, parents can
be powerful models of positive criticism. A clear and
active example of desired behavior is much more
meaningful to a youngster than words, particularly
with preschoolers. Words are too easily misunder-
stood, forgotten or, worse yet, resented. But demonstration is usually welcomed and imitated.

Every parent knows how children eagerly mimic
them, from the little girl who puts on her mother's
cosmetics and high-heeled shoes to the little boy who
copies his father's mannerisms.

*Kathy, ten, was almost always late for the
school bus. She lost precious minutes hunting
for the jeans and shirt she wanted to wear; she
had to hunt all over the house for her school
books and homework. Criticizing her for being
"disorganized" seemed to have no effect.*

*One evening Kathy said to her mother, "I
don't know how you manage to wake us up,
make breakfast, get yourself ready, and be off to
work on time every day. I wish I could be like
that."*

*Taking the cue, Kathy's mother showed her
how she planned everything out the night before—setting the breakfast table, putting coffee
in the pot, choosing and laying out her next
day's clothes, placing the papers she would need*

at work in her briefcase. Seeing her mother demonstrate how *to be organized was a real learning experience for Kathy—far more than being verbally criticized for being "disorganized." She very quickly modeled herself after her mother, getting ready the night before, and seldom again missed the school bus.*

Effective models can include friends, teachers, older brothers and sisters—anyone a child likes and respects and who has the positive attributes you wish the child to emulate.

GUIDELINES FOR STRATEGIC MODELING:

1. Choose a model that has status for the child.
2. Be sure the child can perform the behavior that is to be modeled (i.e., the behavior must be age-appropriate).
3. Be sure there is ample opportunity for the child to observe the desired behavior.
4. Frequently pinpoint the specific behavior you want the child to follow. This guards against having the child imitate inappropriate behavior (such as smoking cigarettes because a parent does).
5. Be consistent in modeling behavior. If you are trying to correct a child's manners, for example, you must act properly yourself at all times.
6. Always praise a youngster when he or she successfully patterns behavior after the model.

Using Outside Sources

Young people are often reluctant to accept or act on parental criticism lest it seem to be an admission that they were "wrong." Adolescents are especially touchy about what they see as a "loss of face." To avoid this problem, try to arrange to have the criticism come from an outside source the youngster respects. Here's how one father did it:

Ten days after my son Pat got his driver's license, he got a speeding ticket. A week later he narrowly missed having an accident when he changed lanes without signaling. I warned him about driving recklessly and threatened to take away his "wheels" if he continued to do so. The boy argued that neither the ticket nor the near-accident was his fault.

I knew Pat was proud of his ability to drive, and I knew criticism from me would just make him take more chances. Then I read in the paper that a famous race-car driver, one of Pat's sports heroes, was going to give "good driving" tips at an auto show. I took Pat to the show, where he listened intently to his hero's talk. On the way home my son said, "I always thought racers took chances, but I guess the best drivers are careful drivers."

When the source of a criticism is perceived as someone other than a parent, a youngster can feel he or she is not "giving in" to authority, but rather agreeing with an expert. Pat—instead of seeing himself as obeying an order or yielding to a threat—credited himself for being a responsible person by deciding safe driving was sensible. The outside source may be an expert, a sports star, an entertainment celebrity, a magazine article, a television documentary—anyone or anything which has status in the mind of the youngster.

GUIDELINES FOR USING OUTSIDE SOURCES:

1. Timing is crucial. Don't call upon the outside source immediately after you have criticized a youngster yourself. He or she will see through the gambit, or take it for granted that you are using the source as "evidence" to back up your own criticism. If Pat's father had said, "Hear what the expert said? I *told* you to drive more carefully!" the experience would have been wasted.

2. Work the outside source into the natural flow of events. Avoid the appearance of setting up an artificial situation.

3. Use appropriate outside sources; otherwise the technique may backfire. A mother who thought her daughter's shirts and blouses were too low cut showed her an article quoting a well-known fashion designer. The expert predicted that the newest styles would feature high necklines. "Oh, Mother," the girl said, "nobody pays any attention to *her* these days— she's passé!"

Reversing Roles

Children also resist criticism because they may not be able to grasp your perspective on the importance of the behavior you want them to change. They tend to see a situation only from their own viewpoint. By reversing roles, however, you can sharpen a youngster's understanding of a criticism, establish its validity, and bring about a more receptive attitude. In role switching, you act out the behavior you have been criticizing, while the child acts out your role as critic. One mother found this worked for her:

Dinnertime at our house was turning into a most unpleasant experience. Our two daughters, ten and eight, bickered almost constantly. They played with their food, accidentally "dropped" what they didn't like on the floor, spilled milk because they were careless. Nothing my husband or I said—pleas, threats, promises—had any real effect.

One night I announced we were going to change places. My husband and I sat in the girls' chairs, and they sat in ours. When I put the food on the table, we began to act just as the girls usually did. They watched us in stunned silence for a moment, then complained that we were spoiling dinner for them by the "silly" way we were acting.

"But that's how you two behave every night," *I said. Seeing themselves as others saw them, so to speak, really worked wonders! From then on the girls' table manners improved remarkably. We seldom had to criticize them again.*

Another woman used a variation of the same technique to get her teenaged son to clean up the den after he had friends over for a Saturday night party. "Asking—or ordering—Tim to clear away the glasses and dishes and records had no effect," she said. "When I complained that it took me half of Sunday to straighten out the mess, he said he could do it in half the time. 'Okay,' I replied, 'next time you take my role and I'll take yours. If you don't think my criticism is fair, I'll stop complaining.'

"A few Sundays later I woke Tim up early and told him it was his turn to clean up the den, and that I was going to sleep late, the way he usually did. When I came out of my bedroom at noon, Tim was still putting things away. He gave me a half-embarrassed grin. 'You're right, Mom, it takes forever,' he said. 'I guess it isn't fair to let you do all the work after my party.' "

GUIDELINES FOR REVERSING ROLES:

1. The child must agree to change roles.

2. Discuss your perception of the child's role ("It *is* nice not to have to clean up a messy room") and encourage him to discuss his perception of your role ("I didn't know it was that much work"). The exchange of insights helps to resolve the criticism intellectually as well as behaviorally.

3. Role reversal is more effective with older children and adolescents; preschoolers are usually too egocentric to play the game properly.

4. Don't switch roles if the exchange would create too much stress or anxiety for a youngster, or if it could be interpreted as a punishment.

Using Analogy

Criticism is more effective when you are able to relate the criticism to a significant previous experience which the youngster has found productive or rewarding. He or she will feel less defensive about accepting the criticism since it does not involve an actual change in behavior, but merely the repetition of what has successfully been done in the past.

Take the case of a bright student who is getting poor grades in chemistry because he is not making the effort to study hard enough. Criticizing the youngster for poor work habits, or insisting that he or she study longer, is not likely to be effective. A parent might better make an analogy, say, with the time the youngster was trying to make the school tennis team: "Remember last spring when you practiced your backhand every day after school because the coach said it would help you make the team? Well, the extra work paid off, didn't it? You made the team. Every time we want to accomplish something it takes some extra effort, at least at the outset. That's the way it is with a new science, too." It is wise to spell out the analogy for the youngster—but then stop. Don't take that extra sermonizing step: "If you study more you'll do well in chemistry, too." Let the youngster draw that conclusion.

GUIDELINES FOR USING ANALOGY:

1. Sharpen your recall of a child's previous ideas and actions.

2. Use a previous experience you know the youngster will remember in detail.

3. Use an idea you know is or will be rewarding to the youngster.

4. Make sure the child has the intellectual ca-

pacity to draw the desired conclusion. If not, assist him.

Dangle the Bait, Not the Hook

Adults frequently criticize children with barbed questions: "Do you call those hands clean?" "What will *that* accomplish?" "Can't you do any better?" The result, in most cases, is to put the youngster on the defensive, forcing him to justify his behavior. As we mentioned in an earlier chapter, humanistic therapist Fritz Perls has said that if you turn a question mark on its side it becomes a hook, and that when you ask critical questions you may be "hooking" the other person into defensive behavior.

Turning a question "sideways" in your mind before you ask it can help you to see whether you are throwing out a "hook." Take the case of a teacher criticizing a youngster's poorly organized history homework. Here is one way to do it:

> TEACHER: Why did you put the section about exploration in the last three pages?
> STUDENT: Well, I thought. . . .
> TEACHER: But didn't you stop to consider . . . ?

The questions are "hooks" because the teacher *knows in advance* that the answer is virtually certain to be defensive or incorrect. The end result can only be that the teacher must provide the correct re-

sponses, and the student, instead of profiting from
the critique, must experience a sense of helplessness
and failure.

But suppose the teacher had asked: "Can you think
of how the section on exploration might have been
tied in more effectively to the rest of your report?" In
that case the student would have been stimulated to
reassess his homework, and able to feel that he was
in fact constructively solving the problem.

In another instance a college student unable to get
a summer job was criticized by his father this way:
"How come you're the only kid I know who can't
find work? Are you trying hard enough?" There are
no constructive answers to these queries, which hit
hard at self-esteem. The man could have dangled
bait instead of a hook: "Can you figure out a way to
present your skills better? Would you like me to help
you put together a resume?" Asking "why" calls for
excuses and defensive explanations. Asking "can"
fosters the search for solutions.

Using questions as bait rather than hooks helps to
preserve a youngster's self-image, encourages him or
her to take responsibility for positive action, and
cultivates practice in problem solving. A parent who
knows in advance the answer to a question can
structure the question so that a youngster can come
up with the "right" response. A parent who does not
know the answer in advance can help to generate it:

> PARENT: Do you think you can manage
> to do all your chores on time?
> CHILD: Gee, I don't know. . . .

PARENT: Well, I don't know either, but maybe we can figure it out and come up with an answer together.

Certainly the parent who commits himself or herself to sharing in the criticism process will be more likely to get an effective result than one who merely dangles a critical "hook" such as, "Why don't you ever get your chores done on time?"

This technique is also useful with very young children if the questions are kept simple. Mother is annoyed because six-year-old Melissa continues to feed table scraps to Fido during dinner even though she has been told many times not to do this:

MOTHER: Melissa, where does Fido eat?
MELISSA: In the yard.
MOTHER: That's right. And is Fido in the yard now?
MELISSA: No, he's under my chair.
MOTHER: That's right. But we don't feed him at the table, do we?
MELISSA: No. (Melissa stops feeding the dog.)

GUIDELINES FOR ASKING QUESTIONS:

1. When you ask a critical question, check to make sure you are throwing out "bait" rather than "hooks."

2. Gear the questions to a youngster's intellectual capacity; otherwise they will block rather than stimulate constructive thinking.

3. If the youngster can't come up with an answer, help out. This protects a child's self-image.

4. Offer positive reinforcement ("Right" . . . "That's good") when a young child gives a constructive answer.

Game Playing

Making a game of criticism is an effective technique for encouraging behavior change in preschoolers. The child "wins" the game by responding positively to the criticism, and the game continues until the new behavior becomes routine.

For example, neither rebukes nor punishments had much effect on five-year-old Danny's bad manners. He rarely bothered to say "please" or "thank you," or display similar common courtesies. Since Danny enjoyed television game shows, his parents created their own version of "Password."

> DANNY: I want some more milk!
> PARENT: What's the password?
> DANNY: Please. I want some more milk, please.
> PARENT: You win. Here's your milk. What's the password now?
> DANNY: Thank you.
> PARENT: Good, you win again.

The same technique can be applied to almost every situation. When Danny tries to squeeze between his parents to go outside, they say: "What's the password?" "Excuse me." "You win. Go ahead and play." It is important for Danny to hear the positive reinforcement, "You win," each time. But when Danny has incorporated good manners into his behavior, his parents need not always respond that way: "Can Johnny please come over to play?" "I'm sorry, but we have other things to do today."

Another way to criticize via game playing is for the parent to demonstrate inappropriate behavior and have the child play the part of the critic:

> PARENT (washing hands): Watch me and tell me what I am forgetting to do.
>
> DANNY: You're not using soap, just water.
>
> PARENT: That's right, you win.

One family plays the game of "expert" as a substitute for criticism: "After our children brush their teeth we make believe we're the dentist and we 'check' their work. 'You did a good job here' or 'You missed this spot,' we'll say, while actually we are doing some rebrushing. The game works with any number of things—tying shoelaces, putting away books and toys, making beds." As with some of the other special techniques, this one is geared primarily toward making the criticism effective (encouraging behavior change) while being careful to protect the child's self-image.

GUIDELINES FOR GAME PLAYING:

1. Parents must be consistent and use the game in all appropriate situations.

2. Keep the game on a "fun" level, and make

sure it always ends with positive reinforcement for the child.

   3.   Make sure the game is structured so the child will "win." If a youngster doesn't know the "password," for example, the parent can supply it and then repeat the question.

The Friendly Bet

According to the late Jean Piaget, an authority on child development, challenge is a key factor in promoting emotional and intellectual growth. Without some imbalance between a youngster and his or her environment, Piaget said, there is little motive for change and improvement.

   The technique of the friendly bet makes use of this theory by generating a mild imbalance: Can a child do something he or she has not been doing? The "bet" is an entertaining way of setting up the stress of imbalance, thus challenging both the child's competitive sense and the need to master one's environment.

   Let's go back to the example of the youngster who leaves her toys scattered about. Instead of criticizing with "hooked" questions ("Why can't you put your things away?") or threats ("If you don't put your things away, I'll. . ."), a parent offers a friendly bet: "I wonder how quickly you can put your toys away. I'll bet you can do it in five minutes!"

   Most children will say "Watch me!" and enjoy trying to beat the time limit. But however long it takes, the parent must follow up: "That was really fast. But if we practice, I'll bet you can put the toys away even faster." That generates a new imbalance. By saying "you can do it even faster," the parent implies the child will ultimately succeed, thus providing additional motivation. Finally, the phrase "if *we* practice" makes the child feel that he or she is not in this all alone, that the parent is an active part of the criticism process.

That second version of the friendly bet has an added advantage because it focuses on competitiveness *within oneself*. There is no fear of being unfavorably compared to some other youngster— "Can I do it quicker than Johnny?" "Is somebody better than I am?"

Still another version matches child against parent: "I'll bet I can put these toys away just as fast as you can." The youngster will usually reply, "No you can't, I'll beat you!" The parent can move slightly faster than the child's normal pace, yet still let him or her "win." The youngster feels successful and competent—but has also responded effectively to the implied criticism.

Remember, the basic criticism model challenges a parent with this question: *How can I communicate to my child that he must learn to put his toys away, that he must learn to be neat and organized?* Helping the youngster to respond positively— "Let's see who can do it quicker" —gets the parent behaviorally involved in the criticism process. This is far different from the parent who says, "Let me see if you can put your toys away correctly." That statement sets up a performance task for judgment rather than a competitive challenge, and can stimulate fears of failure: "Can I do it? Will Daddy still love me if I can't?"

GUIDELINES FOR THE FRIENDLY BET:

1.   The "bet" should be challenging but not overwhelming. Make sure the child is old enough to do what you want done. Conversely, the challenge must not be too simple or the youngster will not be sufficiently motivated to accept it.

2.   Avoid challenges that may arouse anxiety ("What if I fail?"), since this may make a youngster afraid to try.

3.   Watch the tone of voice in which you suggest the bet. Don't make it sound as if the child has to "prove" himself or herself.

4.   Teachers who use the "friendly bet" technique should take into account a child's background. Some youngsters do not grow up in a cultural environment that stresses competitiveness.

Using "Build-Ups"

You can increase a youngster's willingness to accept criticism by prefacing it with a compliment—and then linking the behavior you are praising to the behavior you are criticizing.

The key element in a "build-up" is that the compliment or praise *must* be genuine, must indicate your awareness that something the youngster has done or is doing deserves credit. Children are not stupid. They recognize insincere praise as the manipulative "buttering up" that it is. The result is to harden a child's attitude toward criticism and reduce the parent's credibility.

Larry H., sixteen, spent many hours in his father's basement workshop. Mr. H., a skilled craftsman, was pleased that his son was learning to use tools skillfully and to build useful objects. But he was increasingly irritated because the boy seldom neatened the workshop or put away tools when he was through with them. Mild criticisms had produced little response, and Mr. H. didn't want to reprimand the boy severely lest he lose interest in woodworking altogether. He wanted to raise the issue in a way that would not affect Larry's liking for the hobby, yet would get him to leave the workshop in good condition.

The father achieved this, finally, by complimenting Larry on the care he took of his own possessions: records and stereo, bike, sports equipment. "It's very responsible of you to take such good care of your things," the father said. "I think that's really great. I'd appreciate it if you would display the same attitude about my workshop equipment."

GUIDELINES FOR USING BUILD-UPS:

1.   The compliment should be for something that is important to the youngster. Larry took care of his possessions because they meant something to him. Praising him for, say, keeping the bathroom neat would be ineffective as a build-up if he did that only

because he had to. Know what your child takes pride in doing.

2. The compliment must not only be sincere, but able to be linked directly to the criticized behavior. A non sequitur such as, "Your grades were excellent, now please keep the workshop orderly," would be ineffective.

Spotlighting Consequences

Protecting a youngster's self-image is another important factor in making him or her receptive to criticism. Spotlighting the possible long-term consequences of unsuitable behavior may help a child to understand that if it continues, it will be to his own disadvantage.

> *Eleven-year-old Sam's parents were distressed because Sam had trouble making friends in his new school. From what they observed, and from what teachers reported, the main reason was that Sam was a braggart and a show-off.*
>
> *Sam's parents realized that his behavior signaled his own insecurity, but they could not expect him to understand or accept that insight. Criticizing his actions would be ineffective. Instead, they discussed with Sam what he would not get—friends, attention, respect—if he continued his show-off behavior. They focused on the future consequences of his behavior.*

Most youngsters will not see highlighting the possible consequences of a behavior as a threat or command from the parent, because the parent has nothing to do with the consequences. Since, in Sam's case, it is his own behavior that produces the consequences, he is in control of what will happen. Similarly, the parent of the reckless teenaged driver we referred to earlier might find this criticism technique effective: "If you don't drive more carefully, the motor vehicle department will revoke your license."

GUIDELINES FOR SPOTLIGHTING CONSEQUENCES:

1. Don't let this technique start an argument. The critic must maintain a neutral stance: "This is what your classmates will do—not me."

2. Emphasize that while the consequences are possible, they do not *have* to occur if there is a change in the child's behavior.

3. Make sure that the consequences you point out are important to the youngster rather than to you.

4. Keep your comment brief so it does not sound like a "lecture."

5. This technique is best used with children eight or older; they are better able to connect current behavior with future consequences.

Using Humor and Paradox

The tensions that accompany giving and taking criticism can be reduced by a touch of humor. Since much of humor is spontaneous, when and how to use this technique depends on the course of events and the ability of a parent or teacher to mesh the two.

To see how humor can serve to make a critical

point, let's go back to Melissa, the little girl who fed scraps to her dog during dinner. One evening when the family had guests, Melissa continued to take morsels from her own plate and give them to the animal. Rather than create a scene by removing the dog or chastising the child, her father said: "Melissa, I think Fido is old enough to cut his own food." While everyone laughed, including the child, her father made sure she understood the point he was making: "You know Fido has his own dish outside, and you can feed him there when it is time for him to eat."

Another device for linking humor and criticism is what may be called the "absurd paradox." By encouraging to the point of absurdity the behavior you want to change, you are putting it in its proper perspective. Some counselors now use "paradoxical therapy" to deal with certain clients. A couple who cannot stop arguing, for instance, may be instructed to argue with each other without fail at least four times a day. Since clients at first tend to resist a therapist's efforts and suggestions, the couple is more than likely to stop arguing altogether. Here is an example of how paradox can be used with youngsters:

> *"When I was teaching my fourteen-year-old to play tennis," one father recalls, "he would get furious with himself every time he hit a bad shot. When that happened he would toss his racquet into the air or hurl it to the ground. I repeatedly warned him that was bad tennis manners, threatened to stop playing with him— but nothing I said had any effect.*
>
> *"Finally I said, 'George, the next time you hit*

the ball out or into the net, I want you to see how far you can throw your racquet. Try to make it land behind my baseline.' My son stared at me for a moment as if I were crazy, then suddenly burst into laughter when he realized the absurdity of what I had said—and the absurdity of his behavior. He never threw his racquet again."

GUIDELINES FOR USING HUMOR AND PARADOX:

1. Make sure your comment is humorous and not sarcastic. Sarcasm makes a youngster feel that you are laughing at rather than with him.

2. Make sure that the seriousness of the criticism is not undermined by the humor.

Giving Permission to Fail

Sometimes the most effective criticism is no criticism. You can often enlist a youngster's cooperation in changing behavior by acknowledging that every-one—yourself included—occasionally makes mistakes, behaves badly, fails at a task. Writes psychologist Peter Madden:

During my years as a science teacher I had count-less experiments and demonstrations that wouldn't work. These failures were invariably met by gales of laughter, occasionally derisive, which seemed to be the children's way of saying, "Well, teacher, how does it feel to be like us?"

My response to their hilarity was usually to join in and have a good laugh at myself and the mess I had made. Then I would generally respond, "OK, I guess that flopped. Let's clean everything up, figure out what went wrong, and plan something else for to-morrow." What I was really telling them—and more important, showing them—was that a failure was just a failure. Nothing more; nothing less. It was an *act* that I could live with, think about, and use to plan for future action.[11]

A mother tells how her nine-year-old daughter's experiment in baking came out of the oven a gooey mess. "It was impossible to find anything good to say about it," she recalled, "so I said, 'Well, that cake is pretty sad.' For a moment my daughter was close to tears, but then she grinned. We both learned a valu-able lesson. My daughter didn't need empty as-surances, or criticism. She needed permission to fail."

Actress Katharine Hepburn is said to have carried this technique to its ultimate degree when she was filming a scene with two youngsters who were awed to be in a movie with her. The first time one of the boys blew his lines, Hepburn reportedly said, "My fault, my fault." The boy asked, "How could it be your fault? I forgot the line." Replied the actress, "Because I delivered *my* line too fast. That made you forget."[12]

Taking Criticism from Children

Most adults resent being criticized by young people. Parents, particularly, interpret criticism from their children as evidence of disrespect, rebellion, defiance, or a "wise guy" attitude. It is the rare parent who hasn't responded to criticism with "Don't you dare tell me what to do!" or "You'll understand when you grow up." And just as children equate parental criticism with being unloved, some parents take a child's criticism as a sign they are not loved. Children are not able to voice their criticisms diplomatically; they are usually brutally direct. It is little wonder, then, that the whole process is so often destructive and ineffective.

Children's criticisms, however, cannot be ignored. They are motivated by many of the same factors that prompt parents to criticize them: to communicate needs, to change behavior, to gain satisfaction or end dissatisfaction. But children have an additional problem: It is scary and sometimes dangerous to be critical of such a powerful person as a parent. In fact, this problem may persist throughout a lifetime. Think of how difficult it still may be for you, as an adult, to criticize your own parents. No matter how old we get, in that sense at least we remain children.

How can you best respond to a youngster's criticism? To begin with, use the basic skills previously outlined: appraise the validity of the criticism, keep your thoughts and emotions under control. Refuse to accept the stereotyped posture that "I can criticize my kids but they can't criticize me." And be sensitive to the following special guidelines:

Demonstrate your own caring, concern and commitment. Although we can sometimes do two things at once, children are apt to feel that unless you give them your exclusive attention, you are not paying attention to them at all. That is why it is important to stop whatever else you may be doing and concentrate on a youngster's words. Your attention testifies to your caring, concern and commitment.

Help your child clarify what he is trying to tell you. Adults often label a youngster's criticism as "nagging" because either they don't understand or don't respond to the essence of what the child is saying, thus forcing the child to repeat the criticism.

> *"My teenager, Julie, found fault with me because I wouldn't buy her a certain make of jeans," one mother said. "When I explained that since she already had four pairs, I felt she didn't need another, Julie said I wasn't being fair. I couldn't see what fairness had to do with it until, some weeks later, Julie again accused me of being unfair and uncaring.*
>
> *" 'Why am I unfair?' I said exasperatedly. 'Because all the other girls at school are wearing the new style of jeans, and they make fun of me because I don't have any.' I was going to make the usual comment about how I didn't care what the other girls wore when I realized that it wasn't the jeans that were important to my daughter; being accepted by her peers was important. I hadn't heard what she was trying to tell me, and of course she hadn't expressed it clearly."*

One way to help a youngster clarify a criticism is to encourage conversation, rather than cut it off with a

"We'll see," or "Talk to me later," or "I said no, and that's the end of it!" Asking a child to tell you more can help both of you get beyond generalizations to specifics.

A second way is to be sensitive to the youngster's feelings: "I understand that you feel unhappy, but try to tell me exactly why." Being sensitive to emotions can give you a better understanding of how important the criticism is to the youngster. Young children often cannot express their feelings adequately in words, and may need your help to do so.

Control your own emotions. Listen to a child's criticism without reacting—verbally or nonverbally—in a threatening or punitive way.

Ask a child what he or she would suggest as a way to resolve the criticism. Too frequently parents and other adults respond to a youngster's criticism in a way that satisfies them, but not the child. Your response to valid criticism should include a change in the criticized behavior, not just a lip-service agreement. Otherwise a child will feel helpless and ineffective.

Show that you listened to the criticism. This goes a step further than paying attention. You need to show your understanding verbally: "I think you have a good point." "I agree with some of what you say, but not all." "I don't see it that way, but I realize that you do." Such remarks help make the criticism process a constructive dialogue.

Thank a youngster for sharing his concerns and feelings with you. When a youngster feels free to express a criticism, it helps him or her to develop

self-confidence. If you accept the criticism in a positive way, a youngster is encouraged to share concerns with you, and to do so in a more constructive
manner each time.

If you forbid a child to criticize you, or show that
you resent such criticism, you are actually teaching
him or her that it is impossible to talk to you about
things that matter. You are also giving the youngster a
poor model for accepting criticism. Your goal should
be to help your child and yourself develop the kind
of relationship in which criticism—in either direc-
tion—will not be a roadblock to intimacy and
growth, but rather a tool to enhance them.

7 | Making Criticism Work on the Job

When former President Carter was faced with a domestic policy crisis a few years ago, he summoned dozens of businessmen, labor leaders, government officials, and clergymen to a "summit meeting" at which he asked for their "bluntest possible" personal criticism of his ideas and leadership qualities. "I am not the kind of person who responds easily to criticism," Carter said later. "I hate to admit that I have defects and that I have made errors. But over a period of a few days I began to see how constructive and helpful this could be to me as President."

For most of us, a strong effort of will is required to accept criticism of our job-related skills or capacities. It is a rare individual who sees such criticism as potentially helpful. More often we gripe about unfair or insensitive superiors and bemoan our inability to criticize them back. Or we grumble about co-workers who are always telling us what we are "doing wrong" but never seem to listen to *our* complaints about *their* work.

Yet if we stop to consider it rationally, criticism on the job can serve several useful purposes. For one thing, it provides feedback about our work performance. For another, it can point out ways in which we can improve that performance and thus increase our value to an employer. For a third, the proper kind of critical give-and-take can help create a work environment characterized by a freer flow of communication among all levels of employees, with a subsequent increase in both efficiency and morale.

But whether criticism on the job actually *does* serve these purposes depends on how it is offered, how one reacts to it, and—a factor that is often overlooked—how well one understands the differences between a work setting and the other settings in which criticism occurs.

One of the first criteria for responding to criticism on the job is to distinguish criticism *of work* from criticism *at work*. The latter occurs in a job setting but has nothing to do with job performance. It is thus usually neither pertinent nor appropriate, yet because we often fail to separate it from legitimate criticism of work, we may feel we are doing poorly in our job merely because we are being criticized in a work setting. Anne, a 27-year-old fashion coordinator, recalls the time she was assistant to a woman designer:

> *Quite often she would ask me to drive her to a meeting, and then on the way she would comment on how messy my car was, or how careless I was to let my gas tank run so low. Once she asked to borrow a pen, and when I had to rummage in my purse for several moments before I*

could find it, she said that was another example of how personally disorganized I was. There were many similar criticisms, and I began to think I was on the verge of being fired for inefficiency. But eventually I realized that nothing she said had anything to do with my work. I may have been sloppy about my own affairs, but I was never sloppy about my job responsibilities.

Another factor that complicates giving and taking job criticism in a constructive and effective way is that at work each of us is forced into a highly structured "role" with specific boundaries. Even though we have roles to play in other areas of living—as spouse, lover, parent, friend, neighbor, and so on—we are free to vary them from time to time. A lover may be devoted or play at fickleness; a husband may don an apron to cook a gourmet meal, and a wife may go on a business trip. Expanding or changing such roles is no longer considered inappropriate. In fact, it contributes to self-growth. Imagine how emotionally and intellectually restricted we would feel if we were forced to assume the same fixed role day in and day out.

Yet this is what we usually must do on the job, since most of us work in settings based on an organizational hierarchy. Each person has a specific niche in that hierarchy and a specific daily task to perform. As a result, each of us has a certain amount of what may be called "work power"—the ability to influence or to make decisions for other people.

If, for example, the head of the typing pool in an office decides to change job schedules, and there are ten employees in the pool, that decision will affect all ten. If the head of clerical services decides to reorganize the entire department, scores of people in addition to those in the typing pool will be affected. Clearly the clerical department head has greater work power than the pool supervisor. Theoretically, work power increases as one moves up in an organization's structure. (But, as we shall see, it can sometimes be a tricky business to assess who has work power over whom.)

Those who have greater work power than we do are our superiors; those whose work power is less than ours are subordinates; those whose work power is more or less equal to our own are our peers. Work responsibilities may change; one's position in the hierarchy may change as a result of promotion; but we still function within the basic superior-peer-subordinate structure.

The structure itself has an unfortunate effect on the giving and taking of criticism. We have come to take for granted certain "rules" about criticism on the job. Traditionally, these rules say, one does not criticize a boss, nor does a boss feel obliged to listen (much less respond) to criticism. But while a boss is free to criticize others, he or she may hesitate to do so, perhaps to preserve a "good guy" image, or, on a more practical level, to avoid alienating indispensable employees.

Similarly, a subordinate is supposed to accept criticism even when he or she feels it is unfair or invalid on the theory that subordinates "have to" accept criticism (or quit their jobs). And peers at work usually hesitate to offer even helpful criticism to one another because they think, *How can I criticize someone who doesn't work for me!*

The goal of this chapter is to facilitate the criticism process between and among superiors, peers and subordinates. We will suggest specific techniques for each relationship in the work structure—i.e., superior criticizing subordinate, peer criticizing peer, and subordinate criticizing superior. A special section will focus on how to deal with particularly difficult situations involving job criticism. Although all these techniques are grounded on the basic model for giving and taking constructive criticism, we will concentrate on how to give criticism, since that is the major problem in the work setting.

Giving Criticism at Work

Criticism on the job is primarily concerned with communicating evaluative information. To be pertinent, the criticism must relate either to work results or to things people do (or fail to do) that directly affect work results.

Minimize as much as possible the impact of the pecking order on criticism. You do not want anyone to respond to criticism just because he or she is low in the hierarchy, but because that person perceives it as helpful. Similarly, you do not want anyone to reject criticism just because he or she has a high-level job. Constructive job criticism should provide a supportive climate that enhances productivity and morale. Awareness of the concepts of work structure and work power can help prevent them from becoming obstacles to effective criticism.

Be sensitive to the environment. The setting in which you criticize a peer, superior or subordinate affects not only the impact of your words but also the impression you create. For example, a secretary criticized by her boss in front of her peers will probably be embarrassed and angry; instead of focusing on the content of the criticism she will more likely be concerned about what her peers are thinking. A boss who criticizes a subordinate in front of other bosses—his peers—risks having them wonder if he or she is a competent manager. Remember that what may be an appropriate environment for criticism in one situation may not be appropriate in another. Select a setting in which you feel the other person will be most receptive to the criticism.

Make sure job criticism is based on objective facts rather than subjective perceptions. Workers often feel criticism is invalid because it is inaccurate. "My boss chewed me out recently because he claimed that my sales reports are always late," a salesman said. "That's nonsense! I admit that particular report was late—but it was the first time I was late in the past year. He's just trying to find something wrong with my work because he's afraid I'm after his job."

Objective criticism also reduces the likelihood of disagreements. If a supervisor tells a secretary, "You are typing too slowly," the typist may well reply, "What do you mean, slowly? I type as fast as anyone else in the office." But if the supervisor says, "You type thirty words a minute and that's below our minimum standards," the typist can hardly argue.

Never forget that the person you are criticizing has invested emotional energy in his or her work, and criticism of it is often seen as an attack on his or her ego. Management consultant Dr. Robert Bramson, who conducts seminars on how to deal with difficult people, tells of a woman whose boss frequently and brutally criticized her in front of her co-workers. Finally, Bramson recalls, the woman made an appointment to speak privately with her boss. She said: "You're my boss and you can say anything you want about my work, but not in a way that leaves me feeling worthless." According to Bramson, the boss not only never reprimanded the woman publicly again, but gained a new respect for her.[13] Observing simple courtesies is one way of showing sensitivity to another person's feelings. A more productive way is to stress the mutual benefits a criticism may yield when superiors, peers and subordinates work together to achieve their goals.

Criticizing a Subordinate

"I don't understand why my employees feel threatened every time I complain about something," the owner of a small printing business said. "I'm just trying to get this shop to run efficiently."

That boss is making a common mistake. He's looking at job criticism from *his* viewpoint rather than from his subordinates' perspective. Oddly enough, many bosses seem to think (or like to think) that they are *not* authority figures to their employees. But the "we're all one big happy family" attitude is a self-deception. By its inherent nature, the work structure establishes the boss as *the* powerful figure—perhaps, though not necessarily, more knowledgeable and intelligent, but certainly more informed, more experienced, more influential. Criticism from such a person represents a threat to a subordinate's sense of job security, and a blow to his or her self-esteem. Criticism from a boss almost always is interpreted to mean, "I'm in trouble."

Feeling threatened, a subordinate tends to react to criticism in a defensive way—denying it, disagreeing with it, questioning its fairness. Even though the subordinate may inwardly recognize that the criticism is valid, he or she still seeks to "convince" the boss it is *not* valid in order to defuse the threat to security and self-esteem.

The most obvious way for a superior to minimize the idea that criticism represents a threat is to avoid making any remarks that can be construed as threatening. But even when there is no literal "threat" a subordinate may still infer one. The more effective strategy, then, is to try to change the psychological structure of the work relationship—to offer your criticism in terms of useful information that can help the other person to improve job performance.

Another way of perceiving the distinction between criticism as threat and criticism as helpfulness is to analyze the assumptions of two types of job superiors. For convenience, let's call one the constructive "criticizing boss," and the other the destructive "critical boss."

The *criticizing boss* believes that subordinates work best when they see how they can achieve their personal goals at the same time as they are contributing to the organization. This type of boss believes employees respond best when they are actively and intelligently involved in their jobs.

The *critical boss* assumes that subordinates work best when they are insecure about the permanence of their jobs. "If you want them to respond, make them feel that there are plenty of others who could do the job better."

The *criticizing boss* generates in his subordinates an understanding of and commitment to job goals.

The *critical boss* keeps a close watch on subordinates. He or she believes in tight supervision because "they can't do it on their own."

The *criticizing boss* uses criticism to encourage independent thinking, innovation and improvement.

The *critical boss* uses criticism to discourage ideas from subordinates and to keep them from expanding their job roles. He or she is convinced they cannot generate solutions to criticism and must be told what to do and how to do it.

The *criticizing boss* uses criticism as a tool to resolve conflict.

The *critical boss* hopes problems will go away in time. He or she uses criticism to stop conflict rather than to resolve it.

The criticizing boss has four main goals: 1) to break down resistance to the criticism; 2) to actively involve the subordinate in the criticism process; 3) to convince the subordinate that his or her work is important and appreciated; and 4) to resolve the criticism by effectively changing a subordinate's work habits or attitudes.

Here are some techniques by which a superior can achieve these aims:

Show clearly how an effective response to criticism can benefit the subordinate.   It is not always possible to promise a promotion or a raise, but other benefits can be used to motivate a change in work behavior. One department head criticized his secretary for not getting her routine work done quickly enough. "If you can figure out a way to deal with that part of your job more efficiently," he said, "I'll see to it that you get more freedom. You can schedule your own workload, leave early if you've finished everything, or take over some responsibilities that may interest you more, such as researching special projects for me." Using incentives like increased freedom and responsibility builds trust and goodwill between superior and subordinate—two qualities that go a long way toward resolving criticisms. A wise boss knows which incentives are most important to each subordinate.

Emphasize the importance of a subordinate's job.   Making a worker feel needed builds self-esteem; more important, a person who feels his or her work is valuable is likely to respond in a positive way to valid criticism of that work. For example:

> *A veteran trucking company driver had begun to be consistently late in his deliveries. After sev-*

eral reprimands produced no change, the chief dispatcher took a different tack. Instead of threatening to fire the driver, he said, "Look, you may not think your job is important, but the fact is you are probably the key person in this whole company. You deliver the goods—and if you don't deliver them on time, it doesn't matter what the rest of us do. According to your own records, you're running late because of truck breakdowns. But it's part of your duties to make sure your truck is in good mechanical condition before you take it out. Your job is too important to the company to risk getting behind schedule. Now, this isn't just a pep talk I'm giving you. I want you to know how serious the problem is, because making deliveries on time is essential to the company's success. In a way, all our jobs depend on you. So can I count on you to check your rig more often?"

In another instance, a patent attorney said that the most difficult job criticism for her to give was to ask her secretary to correct typing errors. When we asked why, she replied, "Well, it's such a menial task. Judy probably resents having to do that kind of work over." There's a warning there for all bosses: never think of any subordinate's job as "menial." If you convey that impression to subordinates, they will likely assume that the work they do *is* unimportant—and that any criticism of it is also unimportant. There is little motivation for change.

The patent attorney could have told her secretary, "Judy, the letters you type reflect the way we conduct our business in this office. If they have mistakes, people will think we're sloppy about everything we do. When I ask you to retype a letter I'm not trying to irritate you, or show you up. Those letters convey our image to clients, and that image depends on you."

It is important not just to *say* a subordinate's work is valuable; explain *why* it is, and how it fits into the overall image and function of the firm.

Seek out the subordinate's evaluation of the situation you are criticizing. It is always important to know the other person's perception of a problem situation. It shows that you respect other opinions, and that you expect the subordinate to take part in resolving the criticism. It also indicates that your own ideas are not fixed, that you are willing to learn from others. As a result, a subordinate's responses to criticism are more likely to be explanations and suggestions for improvement rather than denials or excuses.

Enlist the subordinate's aid in dealing with the criticism. For work behavior to change, the new plan or regimen must make sense to the employee if he or she is to be motivated by it and committed to it. That's why it is essential first to ask a subordinate how the criticism can be dealt with, and then to involve him or her in the specific implementation of that plan.

Remember that nobody is perfect. Bosses may hope for perfection, but they certainly should not expect it. Just as superiors make mistakes from time to time, so do subordinates. Unrealistically high expectations for work performance are merely going to trigger a flow of unproductive critical comment. The boss who is tolerant of the occasional error shows an empathetic understanding of human shortcomings and a sensitivity to the pressure of job demands. And since rational expectations lead to reasonable work standards, they contribute indirectly to a lessening of unproductive criticism.

Criticizing a Peer

A peer is someone whose work power is seen by both of you as equal to your own. Since the hierarchy of organizational structure places you both at more or less the same job level, you are also both presumably at the same level of competence and status. As a result, it is assumed that you do not have the "right" to criticize each other. Human nature being what it is, however, such a state of affairs is illusory. Criticism between peers is a common occurrence. In many instances it creates rivalries and antagonisms that benefit no one; but when carried out astutely it can accrue to the advantage of both persons.

Perhaps the biggest obstacle to overcome in order to effectively criticize a fellow worker is to convince him or her that you are not intruding into his or her "territory." Even though your criticism may be intended as helpful, the other person may think you are sticking your nose into something that is none of your business—that you are "playing boss." Therefore, you will want to *relate yourself* to the criticism so that peers hear it as an offer to cooperate rather than as an order, and so that they see it as "some of your business" rather than "none of your business."

A second obstacle is the sense of competitiveness that often arises between peers. Competition tends to set up what psychologists call a "zero sum" situation, in which the winner takes all and the loser gains nothing. That is why criticizing peers in a way that makes them feel you are competing with them for advancement or recognition simply makes them more likely to reject whatever you say. Consider what happened when two junior advertising copywriters were assigned to dream up a new campaign concept for one of the agency's accounts:

"Every time I came up with an idea," one of the copywriters said, "Steve managed to find something wrong with it. Of course we both were playing the same game—every time Steve made a suggestion I found a reason to downgrade and reject it. We were not only competing to see who could come up with the better idea, we were competing to see who could find the most flaws in the other fellow's idea. Obviously we didn't make much progress. Eventually the copy chief took us both off the assignment, and it was a long time before we got another chance to show what we could do."

Peers communicate competitiveness when they stress "ownership" of an idea or a project—referring to "my idea" as opposed to "your idea," or "the way *I* do that job" versus "the way *you* do that job." Peers also set up a competitive climate for criticism when they take the attitude that there is not enough credit for both persons to share.

Blaming one's peers for one's own errors or failures on the job is a third obstacle to constructive peer criticism. How many times have you heard someone say, "I would have gotten that report out by the deadline but Jim didn't get the statistics to me on time"? Perhaps Jim didn't carry out his part of the assignment on schedule, but putting all the blame on him merely sets up a destructive accusation-defense situation. Jim is hardly likely to accept the criticism, for if he does he is implicitly accepting responsibility for the breakdown of the entire project. The only way Jim can protect his position (and his self-image) is to reject the criticism out of hand.

All of these obstacles have a common denominator: they lead to arguments. When superiors criticize subordinates, or when a subordinate criticizes a superior, an argument is rare; in the former instance the criticism cannot well be rejected, and in the latter it can either be rejected or ignored. But because peers have equal work power, arguments are not only permissible but expected. Yet, when both parties have their personal worth at stake, they are not likely to give or take criticism in a useful way.

Since "a man convinced against his will is of the same opinion still," we need to use techniques that will enable us to offer criticism to a peer without starting an argument.

Couch your criticism in terms of a common goal. Use words that stress cooperation rather than competitiveness or blame. For example, "*We* can get the report done quickly if *you'll* firm up the statistical data while *I* edit the text," is bound to be more effective than "Unless *you* get moving faster on the statistics *I* won't be able to finish the report on time." Emphasizing the common goal, and using words like "we" and "our" that imply a sharing of credit for a job well done, reduce the harmful implications of competition.

Show how a peer's work performance affects both of you.   When you stress a common goal you are deleting implications of blame from your criticism. When you include yourself in a peer's actions you are showing how both of you can benefit if he or she acts upon your criticism. In effect, you are convincing the other person that what may seem to be "none of your business" is indeed your business.

This technique is particularly useful when two persons work together as a team. For example, your partner is consistently late to staff meetings, leaving you to stumble through your presentation without all the pertinent facts. Instead of saying, "Terry, you're never on time and it makes me look like a fool," your criticism would be more effective phrased something like, "Terry, it's important for both of us to be at the staff meetings on time. If one of us is late it creates a bad impression and we both suffer."

Agree with a peer's behavior but point out that others—more important than yourself—probably won't.   Martha worked as a secretary to an editor before she was promoted to an editorial assistant's job. She noticed that Joanne, her successor, did not type up the notes she took at editorial meetings. Martha did not want to "play boss" and tell Joanne she was supposed to type those notes. But she knew that the editor wanted them in that form. Martha got her criticism across by agreeing with Joanne: "I've noticed that you file meeting notes without typing them. I agree that's easier and just as accurate. I used to do the same thing until I learned that the boss gets very annoyed if those notes aren't typed. I think you'll save yourself a lot of trouble if you take my suggestion."

This technique made Martha an ally rather than a critic of Joanne. If Joanne was going to argue about the matter, she would have to do so with the editor. Similarly, you can increase the chances of a peer's being receptive to criticism if you put it in terms of sharing what you have learned to be a better approach to a task. Try prefacing your comment with remarks such as, "That's how it looked to me, too, until . . . ." or "I used to do it that way too, but . . . ."

Criticizing the Boss

It is a delicate matter to criticize someone who has "work power" over you. Superiors often say, "Feel free to tell me anything that's on your mind," but most of us know better than to make too much use of that offer. The fact is that while they want to keep lines of communication open between themselves and their employees, bosses expect that communication to be concerned chiefly with information related to the employee's work—not their own.

Superiors simply do not expect to hear criticism from subordinates. (We use "criticism" in this section specifically to mean suggestions for change in the workplace. The point is not whether superiors *should* listen to it, but whether they expect to.) Bosses may be willing to accept criticism from those whom they feel are equally or more experienced, equally or more responsible. But since subordinates are not thought to be so qualified, bosses are often unreceptive at best, or antagonistic at worst, to any criticism from them.

Nevertheless, there are times when it is useful or necessary to criticize a superior. How can you best go about it?

One tactic is to minimize the boss's expectation that you should not, or are not qualified to, criticize him or her. One way to do this is to take on, over a period of time, enough additional responsibilities beyond your normal duties so that the boss thinks of you as qualified for a higher work level. Another way is to make yourself available to the boss—which means, of course, making *him* available to *you*. You can accomplish this by suggesting that he schedule a specific time each week or month to meet with you; or by simply letting him know that you are available should he want to talk with you.

Further, cultivate a friendly relationship with your superior without being sycophantic about it. A friendly relationship does not mean seeking to be "friends"; it does mean asking for advice, showing respect for a boss's opinions, not carrying a chip on your shoulder about his or her authority. Many superiors discourage this kind of interaction because they think subordinates do not value what they have to say. Showing that you do value your boss's comments is likely to foster a mutually respectful relationship between you.

Second, assess whether and when it is appropriate

for you to criticize your superior. To do this you will have to ask yourself some questions:

—Do I have a direct line of communication with my boss? If you have to go over someone else's head to reach him, both your immediate superior and your ultimate superior are going to be embarrassed and irritated. You're through before you start.

—Does my supervisor's work affect the results of my work, or that of my subordinates? To be effective, criticism should be directed at something the boss does (or does not do) that impinges on your own job. For example, if you are supposed to set up a weekly production schedule but your boss consistently fails to give you the input data you need, it is certainly appropriate for you to criticize. It is equally appropriate—although perhaps more risky—to criticize a superior's job-related attitudes if they affect your or the staff's work.

"I once worked for a man who was so secretive that when he went out of town on business he did not let me know until five minutes before he left the office," a magazine editor recalled. "I was supposed to take over in his absence, but it was hard to do that efficiently on such short notice. It meant a frantic scramble for everyone on the staff."

Some bosses are hostile, manipulative, or indecisive to such an extent that they adversely affect work output and morale. It is clearly *in*appropriate to criticize decisions that have nothing to do with you or your job, such as hiring and firing, transfers or promotions of personnel.

—Last, do I know what I'm talking about? You must have facts, figures and examples to support your criticisms. Otherwise you will be labeled a complainer or a troublemaker. As we've said, bosses are not likely to give much credence to a subordinate's criticism to begin with, so it is important to establish yourself as a valid source of criticism.

Once you have decided whether it is appropriate to criticize your superior, the next step is to:

Assess how receptive to criticism you think he or she is apt to be. Again, ask yourself the following key questions:

—Does my boss encourage interaction with employees? You can tell from small but significant clues: whether his office door is kept open or closed; whether he circulates among staff people or keeps himself isolated; whether he schedules meetings at which everyone is free to speak up.

The boss who recognizes the importance of maintaining informal contacts with employees is indicating that so far as he or she is concerned, the boundary lines between superiors and subordinates is permeable. However, be wary of jumping to conclusions about a boss who "socializes" with subordinates. Some standoffish superiors are quite willing to listen to meaningful criticism, while some seemingly free-and-easy ones are not open to it at all.

A boss who *says* he is available but consistently makes it difficult for you to talk with him ("I can only give you five minutes" or "I won't be free till Friday at 10 o'clock") makes the criticism process an uneasy one for a subordinate. What initially may have been a simple observation tends to become exaggerated, because the boss—having set aside his time—may expect to hear something of great importance.

—Is my superior rigid in his or her thinking, or willing to solicit ideas from subordinates? Is his or her conversation studded with flat assertions and demands, or is it marked by a flexible approach to possible change?

"When I went to work as assistant merchandising manager in a medium-sized department store," a woman said, "I found the methods of operation were ten years behind the times. I went to my boss and suggested a number of changes. He told me that when he retired I could do whatever I wanted, but as long as he was in charge we'd do things his way. He vetoed every suggestion I made with the same words: 'I've been here fifteen years with no complaints, so why should I listen to you?' "

Careful assessment of your superior's receptivity to criticism is doubly important. A close-minded boss may interpret your critical comments as an attempt to embarrass him, or to impress higher-ups, or even to maneuver for his job. A boss whose attitude is more flexible hears constructive criticisms as suggestions that may help the organization.

Once you have judged that it is appropriate to voice a criticism to your superior and decided that he or she is likely to be receptive to it, how do you then make sure that your criticism will be seen as constructive and that your boss will respond to it in a positive way?

Acknowledge that he or she is the boss.   Don't try

to prove that you are right and the boss is wrong. A criticism that openly challenges a superior's ability or authority, or which seems to be setting up a power struggle, only makes it more certain he or she will defend the status quo.

Social psychologists have found that an excellent way to get your ideas accepted is to put them in the form of a "two-sided" argument. Summarize the current situation first and then make your constructive criticism, emphasizing that it may provide an alternative. By presenting both sides of the case you are, in effect, acknowledging your boss's position and defusing his or her need to defend it.

Assume, for example, that you are a middle executive in a manufacturing plant that operates around the clock. Current practice is to notify workers of shift changes only two days before they go into effect. You know that most employees resent this because it does not give them enough time to rearrange their own and their families' schedules. You plan to criticize this procedure at a management meeting. You could say, "The way shift assignments are made around here is terrible! No wonder employee morale is so low!" But you know what would happen if you said that. Instead, you use the two-sided argument approach: "I realize shift changes can't be scheduled too far in advance because of production factors. But it seems to me that the current situation makes for poor employee morale—and we all know how that can affect productivity. I can only speak for myself, but I would like to suggest that we try to find some way of giving employees more advance notice. It's just an idea I thought you might want to consider."

You have summarized the current situation; presented an alternative; emphasized its advantages; and left the decision to your superiors. The phrase "current situation" depersonalizes your criticism— something is happening but you are not singling out your superiors as having caused it to happen. The phrase "I can only speak for myself" reassures your superiors that there is no conspiratorial "office revolt" under way.

Build up the validity of your criticism. The point here is not so much to present *yourself* as a valid source of criticism as it is to present your *information* as valid. Some ways you can do that include: citing authoritative sources, submitting supportive data, quoting experts in the field, showing reference material to your superior. The aim is to maximize the significance of your information and minimize the superior-subordinate relationship. Instead of coming on as a critic, you are sharing valuable data that relates to *both* your jobs. Your superior, instead of having to accept or reject a criticism, is now in the face-saving position of merely having to evaluate the information you supplied.

Ask for your boss's help in resolving the criticism. This immediately makes you an ally of your superior. For example: "I'm having trouble planning your appointment schedule because I don't know when you are going to be available," a secretary said to her boss. "I'm not sure how I should handle this. Can you give me some ideas?"

When you ask for help you are bringing several positive factors into play. You are: showing respect for your superior's opinion; avoiding any implications of a power struggle; acknowledging his or her right to make decisions; showing that you feel comfortable enough with your superior to ask for help; and virtually forcing him to pay attention to your criticism by setting up a problem he or she must resolve.

Special Situations

For the past two years we have been asking men and women who attend workshops in criticism skills what is the most difficult kind of criticism for them to give or to take in a work setting. Half a dozen representative situations are mentioned repeatedly in one form or another. The six case histories which follow typify these situations. While the tactics for dealing with them vary in each instance, they share a common denominator for basic strategy. It is to deemphasize verbal communication and to focus instead on action that can resolve the dilemma by bringing about a change in the other person's behavior.

SITUATION: You are an assistant to a bank manager. Your superior sees only what he thinks are your faults, and he constantly criticizes you in a destructive way. You are hard put to restrain your anger and resentment, and your self-image is taking such a beating that you are starting to wonder if you are incompetent at your job.

GOAL: To make your superior realize that some of his destructive comments may be unfair or invalid, and to alert him to the merits of your work.

ACTION: To devise a "structure" for the criticism process that will oblige the bank manager to take a broader view of your work and thus recognize its overall merit.

You ask him if the two of you can meet privately each Friday morning to review your week's work. At the first meeting you say, "I try to do my best in my job, but I'm beginning to feel ineffectual because you constantly find fault with what I do. I'd appreciate it if you could hold all your criticisms for this weekly session. Then you could tell me what I'm doing that displeases you, how I can improve, and perhaps comment on ways in which I am already working effectively."

At first the bank manager has a long list of things he thinks you have done wrong. But as the meetings continue he begins to change his tune. "I guess I wasn't aware of how much you really accomplish here," he says. Another time he remarks that he is probably "a bit of a perfectionist" and perhaps expects too much from his subordinates.

In effect, you have helped your boss to change his behavior by "forcing" him to stop pouncing on isolated errors and instead to judge your competence from a wider perspective. Too, the weekly review indirectly influenced the manager to clarify his unrealistic expectations for your job performance. On the other side of the coin, by requesting the weekly meeting you proved you were willing and able to accept negative criticism in a constructive way.

SITUATION: A co-worker in the billing department of your company seems to enjoy "playing boss" and frequently criticizes the way you do your job. Since he is your peer you feel he has no right to do that.

GOAL: To make him stop.

ACTION: You've already tried several tactics—moving your desk further away, ignoring his remarks, showing your displeasure—but none of them has had any effect. Your strategy, therefore, must not be to stop your co-worker from criticizing you, but to make him do so constructively. Just as a jujitsu expert uses an opponent's power and applies reverse leverage to overcome him, so you plan to take advantage of what your peer is already doing.

Instead of resisting his comments, or replying angrily to them, say that you appreciate them because they are "helping you do a better job." Ask open-ended questions which, in effect, criticize your co-worker's criticisms. For example, if he finds fault with the way you are handling an assignment, ask: "How would you do it?" or "What do you think we ought to do next?" This forces him to make a constructive suggestion. If he cannot, then he has to join you in trying to solve the problem and/or stop criticizing you. If he does make a useful suggestion, you will have been helped and can't complain.

SITUATION: You find it repeatedly necessary to criticize your subordinate, a research analyst, because she continually puts off decisions. But she always has an excuse. You know she delays because she is afraid to make a decision. But she defends herself by saying she needs to double-check a fact or figure, or run a confirming analysis. The result is that her reports are never ready when you need them.

GOAL: To convince your subordinate to stop making excuses.

ACTION: You realize the analyst uses various pretexts in order to disown responsibility for her behavior and avoid facing up to a possibly threatening change in the way she handles her job. Your strategy is to protect the woman's self-image and sense of security by *giving her permission* to be wrong at times.

For example, you might say: "I know you have a difficult assignment, and you can't always have your reports done exactly when I need them. And I know that if you're working against a deadline there will sometimes be an error in your analysis. But I'd rather have you make a mistake now and then than have you consistently turn work in late." Since she now knows it is all right to be wrong occasionally, she will no longer need to find excuses for it. And chances are that as she stops worrying about making mistakes, her reports will not only be more prompt but also more accurate.

SITUATION: You have found it necessary to criticize a subordinate frequently for forgetting to put tools away at the end of the workday. He agrees that what you say is right, but does nothing about it.

GOAL: To get the man to act on your criticism.

ACTION: Continued criticism is useless. This person needs your help and commitment to adopt new behavior. You must do something to bring about the change you desire. You might tape a memory-jogging note over the man's workbench; ask him to help you put your tools away, thereby prompting him to do the same; or you may remind him verbally at quitting time. Eventually the man will "learn" to put his tools away without being cued to do so. This strategy requires patience and constant follow-up on your part, and you need to make sure your attitude is helpful rather than nagging or bossy.

SITUATION: Your superior is openly hostile toward you every time you turn in work or make a suggestion. He often shouts at or demeans you in front of others.

GOAL: To set limits for your boss by letting him know that his "work power" over you does not entitle him to embarrass or abuse you.

ACTION: If you try to talk to your superior about his behavior toward you, he may deny that he is hostile or accuse you of being oversensitive. Your strategy must be *not* to get the boss to change his attitude, but to change yours. The behavior of difficult and hostile people usually works well—for *them*. That is why it is up to you, according to management consultant Robert Bramson, to act in a way that will change the nature of the interaction. (Some of his suggestions follow.)

In this situation, you must react to your superior in a calm and dignified way, showing him that you are prepared to stand up for your work and opinions no matter how hostile he is. You can accomplish this by addressing your boss directly, by name or title, and making subjective statements such as "I disagree." "In my judgment, . . ." "Nevertheless, it seems to me . . . ." If he responds by being even more hostile, deliberately break off the conversation. Say, "This is important to me, and I want to discuss it, but not this way. I'll be back in an hour." This may be hard to do at first, but if you hold your ground by concentrating on your own feelings and doing your best to ignore his reaction, you will very likely wear down his hostility in the long run.

If your superior is covertly hostile—if he makes fun of you, is sarcastic, or talks about you behind your back—you can try to force him either to bring his hostility out into the open, or end it altogether. For example, if your boss "jokes" to a colleague that you are "always late for meetings," go to him privately and say, "When you kidded about my being late, I wasn't sure if you meant it as a joke or not. Did you mean it as a joke?" Always end your remark with a question the boss must answer. If he replies, "No, I wasn't joking," at least matters are out in the open. If he says he was, you can announce quietly that you don't appreciate being kidded that way in front of your co-workers. But what you are really telling the boss is that his camouflage isn't working anymore.

SITUATION: Your boss criticizes you for turning a report in late. You know that it was late because your subordinate failed to deliver the statistics for it on time.

GOAL: You don't want to have to take the blame for a subordinate's mistake, yet you don't want to seem to be fobbing it off on someone else.

ACTION: It is an error to focus on the relationship between you and your superior. Making excuses won't help; they are repugnant to most bosses. Besides, the ultimate responsibility to meet deadlines is yours and yours alone. Blaming subordinates will only suggest to the boss that you are not able to get them to perform efficiently.

The appropriate strategy is to agree with your superior, accept his criticism, and keep to yourself the reason the report was late. The problem is not between you and your boss but between you and your subordinate. Use constructive criticism to motivate him so that the incident is not likely to occur again.

8 | Nobody's Perfect: The Trap of Self-Criticism

Long before the psychology of self-esteem taught us how important it is to have a decent opinion of ourselves, Mark Twain summed up the theory's basic principles in a single insightful remark: "A man," he wrote, "cannot be comfortable without his own approval." But it often seems harder to gain that ultimate accolade than to win the approval of others. The harshest criticism many of us receive is the criticism we give ourselves.

In her essay on self-forgiveness author Ardis Whitman says, "We brood over what we've done and what we've left undone; over the hurts we've brought to others and the damage we've brought to ourselves; over . . . the inability to get rid of whatever faults we may have."[14] Most of us are willing to forgive the failings of others. Why can't we forgive our own? To answer that question—to become aware of the dynamics of self-criticism—we must first understand how the relationship between criticism and self-image works.

Paradoxically, one's concept of one's "self" does not develop from the inside out, but rather is fashioned from the outside in. "O, wad some Pow'r the giftie gie us/ To see oursels as others see us!" Robert Burns exclaimed. But that is precisely the way we *do* "see ourselves." It is how we think that we appear to others, and how others judge us, that is largely responsible for the self-image we construct. And because we internalize the standards and opinions imposed on us by others, we tend to take on their attitudes and measure our own behavior by them.

In an earlier chapter we pointed out how repeated criticism in the formative years of life from those who are emotionally important to us can lead to the development of a poor self-concept. A child who grows up with destructively criticizing parents, for example, is likely to internalize the judgments those parents voice and the way in which he thinks they perceive him. But it is not only the *content* of parental criticisms that is made a part of the self-image. The child is also likely to internalize the criticism *process* he or she has been exposed to, and thus become a destructively self-criticizing adult.

In short, self-critics are simultaneously both givers and takers of criticism, quick to berate themselves in destructive ways and also to interpret that criticism destructively. That is why self-criticism can be doubly damaging unless we understand how to deal with it effectively—how to reject it when it does us a disservice, and how to make use of it when it is to our advantage.

The Fear of Failure

Man has an inherent need to master his environment, to deal with the challenges of living in a competent way. One of the useful purposes self-criticism serves is to help us evaluate our actions so that we can constructively answer that constantly recurring inner question, *How am I doing?* But the person who has internalized a destructive approach to self-criticism sabotages its useful function. He or she has *learned* to do so as a child through years of exposure to negative criticism.

A child, for example, may be rewarded with love and approval for outstanding performance—a fine report card, athletic success, good behavior. But when parents react to that youngster's occasional shortcoming or deficiency with anxiety, disappointment or rebuke, the child will most likely interpret that response as a punishment or rejection. Not surprisingly, such a child becomes especially sensitive to failure, whether real or imagined. He or she actually begins to anticipate failure, to closely monitor his or her behavior to see if it threatens to occur. The child seeks to acknowledge failure before his or her parents do.

This pattern becomes a learned habit. It represents the first characteristic of destructive self-criticism:

looking for defects, anticipating mistakes—in short, focusing on the negatives in one's life. By thus perpetuating a poor self-image, the self-critic blocks possibilities for change and growth. A man, for instance, clings to a relatively secure but dead-end job because he is afraid that if he accepts a more challenging one he may fail. A woman stays in a boring marriage because she fears she isn't clever or pretty enough to attract another man.

Focusing on negatives has two major consequences for thought and action. One is the tendency to jump to the conclusion that a single mistake or failure will be endlessly repeated. When something goes wrong, the destructive self-critic says, *That always happens to me ... I can never do anything right.* This emotional constriction tends to make the self-critic avoid any experience or turn away from any opportunity which does not have a successful outcome firmly guaranteed. Since failure is equated with fear of rejection, he or she forestalls rejection by essaying nothing which might fail. The predictable result is stagnation.

The Need to Be Perfect

A second characteristic of destructive self-criticism is the need to be perfect.

Barbara and Greg gave an elaborate dinner party for twelve guests. All proclaimed the evening delightful and the food superb. But when the last guest had left the hostess collapsed in tears.

"I'm so upset," she said. "The hollandaise sauce was lumpy and the rolls were cold."

"But that doesn't matter," Greg said. "Everything else was excellent, and everyone had a wonderful time."

"That's not the point," Barbara replied. "I wanted it to be perfect."

———

Jason, a law student, ranked seventh in a class of eighty-five at the end of his first year. To his professors' astonishment, he dropped out of school. His reason? "I've always been tops in my class," he explained. "If I can't be number one in law school, then I'm not good enough to be an attorney."

Many men and women think they have failed when they do not live up to their own unrealistic expectations. Though they can almost never meet the rigorous standards they set for themselves, says psychiatrist David Burns, they nevertheless have an "irrational belief that they must be perfect to be accepted." (Or *self*-accepted. A well-known woman writer recently confessed that "sometimes, when I really want to drive myself bananas, the judge inside myself adds that I'm not *self-critical* enough.")

This need to be perfect also stems from childhood experiences of parental criticism. To bolster their own self-esteem, parents often expect a child to achieve results beyond the youngster's desires or abilities. A mother may push her average-student daughter to make the Dean's List; a father may press his athletically uncoordinated son to go out for the varsity football team. Any behavior that falls short of these expectations, no matter how great an achievement in itself, is apt to be considered a "failure" and provoke destructive criticism. Eventually the frustrated youngster decides (again unconsciously) that in order not to be criticized—i.e., rejected—he or she must always strive for and achieve nothing less than perfection.

When internalized in adulthood, this need to be perfect means one has replaced one's parents' unrealistically high expectations with one's own. No matter how well such a person performs, he or she is apt to evaluate that performance in terms of an all-or-nothing self-critical put-down. David Burns singles out such thinking as "perhaps the most common mental distortion" of perfectionists: "They evaluate their experiences in a dichotomous manner, seeing things as either all-black or all-white; intermediate shades of gray do not seem to exist."[15]

In other words, the need to be perfect places a person in a self-destructive double bind. If one fails to meet the unrealistic expectation, one has failed; but if one *does* meet it, one feels no glow of achievement for one has only done what was expected. There is no objective way to measure effort or improvement, no chance to relish success, no reason to build up one's self-image.

"Should" statements are often a hallmark of this

attitude: "It wasn't too bad a job but it *should* have been better." "I didn't get as much done as I *should* have." Such statements are damaging enough when applied to actions, but they can be much more damaging when applied to feelings. Self-critics often disparage themselves for feeling a certain way—angry, hostile, even happy—because they "shouldn't" feel that way. But when we destructively criticize ourselves for feelings, we create a no-win situation. Denying the legitimacy of our feelings inhibits the healthy or necessary expression of emotion; reproaching ourselves for our feelings without reason makes us out to be some kind of villain.

Effective Self-Criticism

Criticizing oneself in positive rather than negative ways involves making use of many of the previously outlined techniques for enhancing the constructive criticism of others. But when you are both the giver and the recipient of the criticism, the process becomes somewhat more complicated. You must first identify and then cast aside the pattern of self-sabotage by training yourself to become an objective observer of your self-critical habits. In effect, you must begin to look at your "self" as if you were another person and your "self" were a separate entity. You must learn to talk about your "self" with yourself. The process may seem awkward at first, but there are ways to facilitate it.

Find out exactly what you are criticizing your

"self" for.   Since the purpose of all criticism is to
provide or elicit information leading to change for
the better, and thus to personal growth, the self-critic
cannot afford generalizations. The person who says
"I'm no good" must ask his or her "self" specifically
what that self is doing or failing to do that leads to
that conclusion. He or she must define precisely
what behaviors need to be changed.

Is one "no good" at one's job? In dealing with
crises? In managing money? In sustaining friend-
ships or love relationships? Most of us would admit
to being ineffective or finding it hard to cope with
one or two such spheres of life. But scarcely anyone
is "no good" at everything, or "no good" in general.
The simple act of discovering that one functions adequately in many areas can go a long way toward dis-
pelling the cloud of negativity that surrounds the all-
encompassing "I'm no good" self-criticism.

Keep a self-criticism diary.   Just as the Criticism
Diary (see Appendix) is useful in analyzing how you
give and take criticism in interactions with others, a
similar record of self-criticisms will help you see
how you deal with yourself. After keeping such a
record for several weeks you will, for one thing, be
able to identify common themes—attitudes and actions for which you most often censure yourself. Are
they very different ones, or are they interrelated? If
the latter, perhaps resolving a basic self-criticism will
also help to resolve one or more of the others.

For example, "I'm too indecisive," and "I'll never
finish decorating my apartment," are clearly con-
nected. Once you are able to change the pattern of

your decision-making process you will find the decorating chores much easier to accomplish. Identifying common themes is important because it helps to keep you from feeling overwhelmed by self-criticisms. At the same time it makes "mental room" for more constructive thoughts.

Another advantage of a self-criticism diary is that it enables you to rank your self-criticisms in order of their importance to you. Suppose you have listed "I smoke too much," "I don't exercise enough," and "I don't keep in touch with old friends." Putting yourself down for all of them, or trying to remedy all of them at the same time, is self-defeating. Rather, decide which criticism is most significant to you—which behavior you most want to change. Then you will be able to concentrate your energy on that specific self-criticism until it is resolved. (Alternatively, you may decide which behavior would be the *easiest* for you to change and resolve that one first. Doing so will reinforce your sense of competency and give you more confidence to tackle the others.)

Build a bridge of "positives" between the giving and taking of self-criticism by holding an internal dialogue with your "self." All too often the critical self-statements we make about ourselves are not subjective *(I made another mistake)* but objective *(You goofed again)*. This is not mere accident or habit of speech. It is clear evidence of how we internalize the process of criticism we were exposed to in our formative years. We are now talking to ourselves the way others talked to us.

However, it is possible to make use of that inter-

nalization by arbitrarily separating the "you" from
the "I"—the giver from the taker of criticism—and
holding a dialogue between the two. The purpose of
the dialogue is to defuse the negative aspects of the
self-criticism and to recast them in a positive and
constructive light.

You do this by making believe you are criticizing
another person for the behavior of your "self," and
by asking "How can I (as giver of the criticism) communicate this information so that I (as taker of the
criticism) will best accept it?" In turn, the "taker"
part of your "self" should listen and respond to the
criticism as you would want another person to do if
you were offering the same criticism.

Such a self-dialogue may at first seem too confus-
ing to carry out successfully. But with practice its effectiveness will become increasingly evident. One
way to structure the internal dialogue is to place two
chairs so they face each other. Assign one chair the
role of the giver of a criticism, and the other the role
of taker. Begin by choosing a self-critical remark you
often make, and then move from chair to chair as
you assume, in turn, the identity of the criticizer and
the criticized person. The goal is to hear yourself—as
objectively as possible—as you give and respond to
the criticism, and to guide the dialogue into a constructive approach to the situation.

Here is an example of how this technique worked
for Stan, a 34-year-old television script writer.

In Stan's case the basic criticism was: *I'm not accomplishing anything in my life.* The italicized comments in parentheses after each of Stan's "giving"

and "taking" assertions show how key principles for improving the criticism process can be applied.

GIVER: You're thirty-four years old and you aren't getting anything accomplished! *(The criticism is wildly overgeneralized and has definite overtones of shaming and blaming.)*

TAKER: Well, you've said that often enough. How about being more specific? What is it exactly that I don't accomplish? *(Uses positive communication technique of asking for more information.)*

GIVER: You're not making any progress in your work, and you never get anything done to make this new apartment livable. *(Still generalizing—note the use of "never"; moreover, the basic criticism has been enlarged to two different criticisms.)*

TAKER: What do you mean, I'm not progressing in my work? *(Probes for more specificity and focuses on one criticism at a time.)*

GIVER: You've been writing the same script for the last six months. You'll never be finished. *(Criticism begins to zero in, but the self-statement is still very negative.)*

TAKER: That's true, I have been working on the same project for a long time. But three months ago all I had done was an outline and a rough draft. Since then I've made significant progress. *(Stan begins to look at some of the positive aspects of the situation that contradict the self-criticism.)*

GIVER: You always say things like that. *(Stan, as giver of criticism, is determined not to acknowledge any progress or let himself off the hook.)*

TAKER: True, but eventually all my projects get done. The script will be finished, too. Besides, while I've been working on it I also turned out three magazine articles and two outlines for other script ideas. *(Stan, as taker, gathers more positive evidence and states it firmly.)*

GIVER: Well, it seems as if you've been stuck on it forever. . . . On the other hand, good writing takes a long time. And you do put in several hours every day at the typewriter. *(Stan's previous response as "taker" has disrupted his self-accusations. What was first offered as fact—"You aren't accomplishing anything"—is now reduced to a hypothesis—"It seems.")*

TAKER: I have to remember that one way or another I get a considerable amount of work done. Other writers may work faster than I do, but I have to be more patient with myself. It takes me longer to get the job done, but it does get done. *(By restating the positives, both sides of Stan's essential "self" are agreeing that at least the work aspect of the original self-criticism is largely invalid and unjustified. Stan's last remarks are positive self-statements that he needs to repeat from time to time in order to stop the self-criticism.)*

GIVER: But you still aren't doing anything about the apartment! *(Reemphasizes negatives; if one avenue of self-criticism fails, tries another.)*

TAKER: Like what? *(Briskly asks for specifics.)*

GIVER: You keep saying you are going to put up shelves, unpack all those cartons, fix the light switch in the study.

TAKER: True, but I haven't had time. I'd rather be working on the script. *(Acknowledges some validity to criticism but offers a reason for lack of action.)*

GIVER: You always say that. But you aren't always writing. Meanwhile, your study is a mess. If you straightened it out perhaps you could work better. How can we make time for you to do that? *(Stan as "giver" makes a constructive suggestion for action that may resolve the criticism. Using the pronoun "we" indicates that he doesn't intend to self-sabotage the venture.)*

TAKER: I don't usually write on Saturdays. Maybe I could work on straightening out the study then, while I watch a football game on television. *(Excuses are dropped because the dialogue is now action-oriented rather than self-critical.)*

GIVER: Why not concentrate on one chore at a time? Which one is most important? *(As an aid to action, tasks are singled out and given priorities.)*

TAKER: Probably putting up the shelves. Once I do that I can empty the cartons and organize my files and my reference books. *(Sees positive results accruing from changed behavior.)*

GIVER: Well, let's focus on one thing at a time. *(Reminds Stan that finishing one task will yield a sense of satisfaction and, in turn, provide the motivation to move on to the next.)* When shall we start? *(Asks for deadline to prevent procrastination.)*

TAKER: This Saturday! The sooner we start, the quicker everything will get done. *(Looks forward to positive results and resolution of self-criticism.)*

This is a relatively simple illustration of an intricate and sophisticated technique. But it does show how holding a dialogue with yourself can generate constructive responses to self-criticism, and help to evaluate (or even deny) their validity.

Take actions that help you to replace self-critical habits of mind with a more positive approach to your self-image. Deliberately seek out and appreciate your strong points rather than focusing on your alleged faults and flaws. Make an accurate assessment of your assets.

"Stretch" yourself to transcend self-critical attitudes and feelings by putting yourself out to help others. Do something you don't want to do or don't have to do. Conversely, be more open to receiving help and emotional support from others.

Surprisingly, it's almost as difficult for most people to accept encouragement or approval as it is for them to offer it; many men and women feel uncomfortable, even embarrassed, when they receive a compliment. But the more you are able to accept emotional support, the more you will be deepening your sense of self-worth. "It is an interesting paradox," says psychotherapist Dr. Richard Robertiello, "that the way to enhance your love for yourself involves accepting admiration from others. In this sense, you are repairing the damage to your self-esteem."[16]

Try doing something that you are not sure you can do well. Many of us are so self-critical that we cut ourselves off from potentially enjoyable or rewarding activities without even trying them. Yet if we *do* try, we often find that they give us pleasure or satisfaction even though we may perform them imperfectly. Consider problems not as signs of failure but as opportunities for success.

Don't berate yourself for not living up to arbitrary standards or other people's ideas. We are each our own measuring stick for our own accomplishments. This is a particularly difficult attitude for many women to maintain in these liberated times. They often criticize themselves for "failing" to simultaneously fulfill the roles of conscientious wife and mother, successful careerist and perfect lover as our society seems to expect of them. But while it is proper to respect the goals of other people, it is not necessary to adopt them as your own—and then criticize yourself for not achieving them.

Look at yourself from time to time through the eyes of those who care about you and love you. You will no doubt find that they have an excellent opinion of you; consider it well deserved.

In this book we have suggested many techniques and guidelines to help make criticism work for you. But more important than any formulas or prescriptions is the spirit in which criticism is offered and accepted. Learning techniques of constructive criticism is one thing; making constructive criticism an integral part of your thinking is far more significant. If we can come to see criticism as a natural form of emotional support rather than emotional attack, we will be better able to give it and take it, to assess it and to benefit from it.

Appendix

Personal Criticism Inventory *

Before you can begin to make consistently productive use of the skills involved in giving and taking effective criticism, you need to examine closely how your thoughts, feelings and actions affect your total response to criticism. Take time now to answer every question on the following *Personal Criticism Inventory* on a separate sheet of paper, using the most appropriate of the following responses: never or rarely; seldom; frequently; almost always. Though there is no overall score or "passing mark," listing your answers in this way will give you a picture of your general response pattern.

Thought Questions

1. When you are being criticized, do you think less of yourself?
2. When you offer criticism, do you think less of the person you are criticizing?

*The standardized versions of the criticism inventories can be obtained from Dr. Weisinger through the publisher.

3.   Do you criticize yourself?

4.   Do the possible consequences of giving criticism prevent you from giving criticism?

5.   When you are criticized, do you understand the criticism?

6.   When you are criticized, do you pay more attention to *how* the criticism is voiced than to *what* is said?

7.   Do you pay more attention to *what* is said than to *how* it is said?

8.   Do you think you are criticized at inappropriate times or in inappropriate places?

Feeling Questions

9.   Do you feel hurt when you are being criticized?

10.   Do you feel depressed when you criticize someone?

11.   Do you feel rejected when you are being criticized?

12.   Do you feel angry when you are being criticized?

13.   Do you feel embarrassed when you are being criticized?

14.   Do you feel embarrassed when you are criticizing someone?

Action Questions

15.   Do you do something about the behavior for which you are criticized?

16. Do you check to find out if the criticisms you give are clearly understood?

17. Do you hesitate to criticize those who are close or important to you?

18. Do you find it difficult to accept criticism from intimate friends?

19. Do you wait for an appropriate time and place to criticize someone?

20. Do you retaliate with a criticism when someone criticizes you?

General Questions

21. Which of the following is most difficult for you? A) Giving criticism; B) Taking criticism. Are both equally difficult? Is neither difficult?

22. What is the most difficult kind of criticism for you to give? Why?

23. What is the most difficult kind of criticism for you to take? Why?

24. Who is the person whom it is most difficult for you to criticize? Why?

25. Who is the person from whom it is most difficult for you to take criticism? Why?

Sexual Criticism Inventory

Answering the questions in the following *Sexual Criticism Inventory* can help partners learn how to offer and accept sexual criticism in a positive and constructive way. The inventory enables you to pinpoint specific sexual criticisms that you find most difficult to give or receive, and it acts as a catalyst in identifying thoughts, feelings and actions that pertain to sexual criticism. Beginning with Question Five, list your responses using one of the following: never or rarely; seldom; frequently; almost always. This will help you to identify your general response pattern.

1.   What is the most difficult sexual criticism for you to give? Why?

2.   What is the most difficult sexual criticism for you to take? Why?

3.   What are your partner's most frequent sexual criticisms of you?

4.   Which of the following feelings do you most frequently associate with sexual criticism? Rejection? Depression? Resentment? Pleasure? A desire to please? Anger? Love? Being pressured? Shame? Being used?

5.   Do you give sexual criticism during lovemaking? Before? After?

6.   Do you give sexual criticism via nonverbal communication?

7.   Does your partner offer sexual criticism nonverbally?

8.   Are you afraid that sexual criticism will hurt your partner's feelings?

9.   When giving sexual criticism, do you compare your partner to other partners you have known?

10.   Does your partner compare you to others he or she has known?

11.   When giving sexual criticism, do you tell your partner only what you do *not* like?

12. Does sexual criticism enhance your sexual relationship?

13. Do you ask your partner for sexual criticism?

14. Does your partner ask you for sexual criticism?

15. Are you sarcastic when you give sexual criticism?

16. Are your criticisms based on your expectations of how lovemaking should be?

17. Do you find you consistently give the same sexual criticism to your partner?

18. Does your partner consistently give you the same sexual criticism?

19. Do you discuss sexual criticisms with your partner at times other than when you make love?

20. When you give sexual criticism, does it tend to lessen the pleasure of lovemaking for you?

21. Do you demonstrate to your partner how to resolve the sexual criticism you give?

22. Does your partner demonstrate to you how to resolve his or her sexual criticism?

23. Are you inhibited in your language when giving sexual criticism?

The Criticism Appraisal Grid

There are six factors, which, when identified, contribute to the appraisal of a criticism. Each of them—importance, source, emotional context, consistency, energy cost and potential benefits—interacts with the other. All must be taken into consideration in deciding whether a criticism is valid and, if so, whether it is worth doing something to resolve it. Using a *Criticism Appraisal Grid* can help you make this judgment.

The Grid allows you to clarify the individual importance of the six factors, to visualize their relative significance, and to assess them as a whole. In effect, the Grid provides a picture of the validity of the criticism as well as a guide to your response. To use the Grid, write down a brief summary of the criticism you received, and then rate each appraisal factor on a scale of one to nine. The higher the rating:

—the more useful or important to you is the information conveyed by the criticism;

—the more credible is the source;

—the more appropriate is the emotional context in which the criticism was delivered;

—the more frequently you hear the same criticism;

—the more energy is required to resolve the criticism by changing your behavior;

—the greater is the potential benefit if you do change.

In general, the higher the Grid ratings are, the more valid the criticism is likely to be, and the more productive a positive response to it will prove. If possible, have a neutral third party rate the factors as well, so that you can test the accuracy of your estimates by comparing them with those of a more objective person.

Bear in mind, however, that the factors may need to be "weighted" since they may vary in importance with different situations and circumstances. For example, in a work environment the source of a criticism may be especially significant even if you score the source low in credibility. Similarly, it may be worth taking positive action on a criticism even though it rates low in almost all areas if it comes from someone important to you, or someone with whom you are in close or frequent contact. Conversely, criticism from a stranger or someone unimportant to you may be considered less valid even though it scores high on the Grid.

On the following pages are three examples of the use of the Grid. The first illustrates a valid criticism, the second an invalid criticism, and the third a criticism that may be valid but is not likely to be acted upon constructively.

CRITICISM: _____

_____

_____

	1	2	3	4	5	6	7	8	9
Importance							X		
Source								X	
Emotional Context							X		
Consistency						X			
Change-Energy Cost								X	
Potential Benefit							X		

ANALYSIS: Factor ratings indicate that the criticism has a high degree of validity. The information it conveyed is significant, the source has considerable credibility, and the consistency score is above average. The cost of making the changes necessary to resolve the criticism is high, but so are the potential benefits. Even though cost slightly outweighs benefits, the ratings of all the other factors suggest making an effort to resolve the criticism.

CRITICISM: _____

_____

_____

	1	2	3	4	5	6	7	8	9
Importance			X						
Source		X							
Emotional Context		X							
Consistency	X								
Change-Energy Cost						X			
Potential Benefit		X							

ANALYSIS: This Grid depicts an invalid criticism. The information has comparatively little significance for the person criticized, or for the relationship involved. It was voiced by a not very credible source in inappropriate circumstances. Few other people have made the same criticism. Change would be stressful and offers few advantages.

CRITICISM: _____

_____

_____

	1	2	3	4	5	6	7	8	9
Importance					X				
Source						X			
Emotional Context							X		
Consistency			X						
Change-Energy Cost								X	
Potential Benefit		X							

ANALYSIS: The factor scores illustrate a frequent dilemma. The criticism would seem to be moderately valid, yet the context and frequency of the criticism are only of average significance. Resolving the criticism would yield few rewards for the high energy cost required. Conclusion: while the criticism may be fair and well grounded, action for change is unlikely.

Personal Criticism Diary

Keeping a "Personal Criticism Diary" is an excellent way to assess the progress you are making in dealing constructively with criticism. If you maintain it faithfully and accurately, it will reflect significant patterns of criticism behavior: whom you criticize most often, and for what; who criticizes you most often, and for what; how you react to giving and taking criticism; and the changes, if any, that you make in response to criticism.

The diary will be most effective if you use it regularly. Take time each day to recall and record the criticisms you gave and received in the preceding twenty-four hours, and to analyze briefly the response as indicated in the following outline.

Date of Criticism: Keeping track of when criticisms were given or received is important. After a few weeks you will be able to see how often a specific criticism occurs and to judge the speed of progress toward change for the better.

The Setting: This shows which environments (office, home, school, mealtimes, social occasions) tend to produce criticized behavior.

Giver/Taker: It helps to document whether you are more often the criticizer or the criticized, and which role is more difficult for you. More important, this category documents the extent to which you consistently criticize, or are criticized by, the same person, and enables you to assess accurately the validity of the source of criticism. Further, it helps you to determine whether most of the criticism you give or take is specifically related to one or two persons, or involves a wider circle of relationships.

Summary of Criticisms: This helps pinpoint the specific attitudes or behaviors that most often result in critical re-

marks. Try to record the criticism as accurately as possible, paying special attention to the exact wording. This highlights destructive tendencies such as generalizing, blaming, making comparisons, and so on.

Thought Responses: Recording your thoughts helps you become aware of the quality of your appraisal of criticism, the self-statements you use, your belief systems, and other contributing factors.

Feeling Responses: This helps you recognize the kind of physiological arousal you experience and the cognitive labels you tend to give it.

Behavioral Responses: Recording how you act after giving or taking criticisms (a problem-solving dialogue or an argument?) helps you judge whether your behavior is mainly constructive or destructive.

Evaluation: Based on the information you have recorded, evaluate the criticism on the following scale:

$$0 \quad 1 \quad 2 \quad 3 \quad 4 \quad 5 \quad 6 \quad 7 \quad 8 \quad 9$$
Counterproductive   Productive

In time these evaluations will provide a graphic display of whether your response to criticism is becoming more positive. By referring to the setting, and the giver or taker, you can also see whether your reaction depends on the kind of criticism offered, the environment and/or the personalities involved.

Reasons: Document the reasons for your evaluation. Did you judge it to be counterproductive because of what was said? Who said it? How it was said? Was it productive because of changes the criticism encouraged? Your answers will give you cues to the areas you need to focus on in future criticism interactions.

Notes

Page

4 1. Stephanie K.D. Hughes, "Criticism and Interaction" (Doctoral dissertation, Boston University, 1974), p. 3.

5 2. Norman M. Lobsenz, "How to Give and Get More Emotional Support," *Woman's Day* (20 September 1977), p. 73.

30 3. Hughes, "Criticism and Interaction," p. 166.

47 4. Ibid., p. 218.

111 5. Richard S. Lazarus, "A Cognitively Oriented Psychologist Looks at Biofeedback," *American Psychologist* (May 1975), p. 558.

128 6. Clifford Sager, *Marriage Contracts and Couple Therapy: Hidden Forces in Intimate Relationships* (New York: Brunner/Mazel, 1976).

132 7. Raymond Babineau, "Development of Sexual Intimacy in Marriage," *Medical Aspects of Human Sexuality* (April 1979), p. 129.

142 8. Carol Tavris, "When to Lie About Sex (And When Not To!)" *Redbook* (October 1978), p. 123.

147   9. Lobsenz, "More Emotional Support," p. 148.

156   10. Charles Schaefer, *How to Influence Children: A Handbook of Practical Parenting Skills* (New York: Van Nostrand Reinhold Company, 1978), pp. 120–121.

178   11. Peter C. Madden, "Teacher, It's OK to Fail Now and Then!" *Today's Education* (March 1973), p. 26.

178   12. Ellen Peck and William Granzig, *The Parent Test* (New York: G.P. Putnam's Sons, 1978).

189   13. Kathleen McCoy, "How to Handle Your Impossible Boss," *Glamour* (September 1980), p. 332.

213   14. Ardis Whitman, "The One Person No Woman Forgives," *Woman's Day* (24 April 1978), p. 74.

218   15. David D. Burns, "The Perfectionist's Script for Self-Defeat," *Psychology Today* (November 1980), p. 38.

226   16. Richard C. Robertiello, "Be Your Own True Love," *Woman's Day* (23 October 1978), p. 90.

Bibliography

Babineau, Raymond, M.D. "Development of Sexual Intimacy in Marriage." *Medical Aspects of Human Sexuality*, April 1979, pp. 128-137.

Bandura, Albert. "The Self System in Reciprocal Determinism." *American Psychologist*, April 1978, pp. 344-357.

Barnabas, Bentley. *Develop Your Power to Deal with People*. West Nyack, New York: Parker Publishing Company, 1971.

Bramson, Robert M. *Coping with Difficult People*. Garden City, New York: Doubleday and Company, 1981.

Brophy, Brigid. *Flesh*. London: Secker and Warburg, 1962.

Burns, David D., M.D. *Feeling Good: The New Mood Therapy*. New York: William Morrow and Company, 1980.

Cooley, Charles. *Social Process*. New York: Charles Scribner's Sons, 1918.

Crowley, Thomas J., and Ivey, Allen E. "Dimensions of Effective Interpersonal Communications: Specifying Behavioral Components." *Journal of Counseling Psychology* 23:3 (1976), pp. 267-271.

Dinkmeyer, Don C., and McKay, Gary D. *Systematic Training for Effective Parenting—Parent's Handbook*. Circle Pines, Minnesota: American Guidance Service, 1976.

Ellis, Albert. *Reason and Emotion in Psychotherapy*. New York: Citadel Press, 1977.

Epstein, Norman, and Jackson, Elizabeth. "An Outcome Study of Short-Term Communication Training with Married Couples." *Journal of Consulting and Clinical Psychology* 46:2 (1978), pp. 207-212.

Erickson, Milton H., M.D., and Rossi, Ernest L., Ph.D. "Two Level Communication and the Microdynamics of Trance and Suggestion." *The American Journal of Clinical Hypnosis* 18:3 (January 1976), pp. 153-171.

243

Feighery, Frank F. "An Experimental Study of the Undesirable Side-Effects of Criticism in Learning Situations." Doctoral dissertation, University of Virginia, 1974.

Gagnon, John. "Does Working Spoil Sex?" *Working Mother,* May 1980, p. 91.

Ginott, Haim G. *Between Parent and Child: New Solutions to Old Problems.* New York: Macmillan Company, 1965.

Goldfried, Marvin R., and Goldfried, Anita P. "Cognitive Change Methods." In *Helping People Change,* edited by Frederick H. Kanfer and Arnold P. Goldstein. New York: Pergamon Press, 1975.

Goldstein, Arnold P. "Relationship-Enhancement Methods." In *Helping People Change,* edited by Frederick H. Kanfer and Arnold P. Goldstein. New York: Pergamon Press, 1975.

Haley, Jay. *Strategies of Psychotherapy.* New York: Grune and Stratton, 1963.

Hewitt, Jay, and Goldman, Morton. "Effectiveness of Various Reactions to a Hostile Attack." *The Journal of Social Psychology* 96 (1975), pp. 245–253.

Hughes, Stephanie K.D. "Criticism and Interaction." Doctoral dissertation, Boston University, 1974.

Jacobs, Marion; Jacobs, Alfred; Feldman, Garry; and Cavior, Norman. "Feedback II—The 'Credibility Gap': Delivery of Positive and Negative and Emotional and Behavioral Feedback in Groups." *Journal of Consulting and Clinical Psychology* 41:2 (1973), pp. 215–223.

Jacobson, Edmund. *Progressive Relaxation.* Chicago: University of Chicago Press, 1938.

Kanfer, Frederick H. "Self-Management Methods." In *Helping People Change,* edited by Frederick H. Kanfer and Arnold P. Goldstein. New York: Pergamon Press, 1975.

Kaplan, Helen Singer, M.D. *The New Sex Therapy: Active Treatment of Sexual Dysfunctions.* New York: Brunner/Mazel, 1974.

Korzybski, Alfred. *Science and Sanity.* Lakeville, Connecticut: International Non-Aristotelian Library Publishing Company, 1933.

Krumboltz, John, and Krumboltz, Helen B. *Changing Children's Behavior.* Englewood Cliffs, New Jersey: Prentice-Hall, 1972.

Lasswell, Marcia, and Lobsenz, Norman M. *No-Fault Marriage.* Garden City, New York: Doubleday and Company, 1976.

Lazarus, Richard S. "A Cognitively Oriented Psychologist Looks at Biofeedback." *American Psychologist,* May 1975, pp. 554–560.

Lazarus, Richard S. *Psychological Stress and the Coping Process.* New York: McGraw-Hill, 1966.

Lefton, Robert E., Ph.D.; Buzzotta, V.R., Ph.D.; Sherberg, Manuel; and Karraker, Dean L. *Effective Motivation Through Performance Appraisal: Dimensional Appraisal Strategies.* New York: John Wiley and Sons, 1977.

Llewellyn, Russell C. "Do Praise and Criticism Have Different Effects on Low Self-Esteem and High Self-Esteem Children?" Doctoral dissertation, Fuller Theological Seminary, 1973.

Levinson, Harry. "The Abrasive Personality at the Office." *Psychology Today*, May 1978, pp. 78–84.

Lobsenz, Norman M. "How to Give and Get More Emotional Support." *Woman's Day*, 20 September 1977, p. 73.

Losony, Lewis. *Turning People On: How to Be an Encouraging Person.* Englewood Cliffs, New Jersey: Prentice-Hall, 1977.

Madden, Peter C. "Teacher, It's OK to Fail Now and Then!" *Today's Education*, March 1973, pp. 25–26.

Masters, William H., and Johnson, Virginia E. *Human Sexual Inadequacy.* Boston: Little, Brown and Company, 1970.

McCoy, Kathleen. "How to Handle Your Impossible Boss." *Glamour*, September 1980, p. 240.

Meichenbaum, Donald. "Self-Instructional Methods." In *Helping People Change*, edited by Frederick H. Kanfer and Arnold P. Goldstein. New York: Pergamon Press, 1975.

Peck, Ellen, and Granzig, William, M.D. *The Parent Test.* New York: G.P. Putnam's Sons, 1978.

Piaget, Jean. *Science of Education and Psychology of the Child.* Translated by Derek Coltman. New York: Orion Press, 1970.

Robertiello, Richard C., M.D. "Be Your Own True Love." *Woman's Day*, 23 October 1978, pp. 88–90.

Robertiello, Richard C., M.D. *Your Own True Love: The New Positive View of Narcissism/The Person You Love the Most Should Be . . . You.* New York: Richard Marek Publishers, 1978.

Rogers, Carl R. *On Becoming a Person: A Therapist's View of Psychotherapy.* Boston: Houghton Mifflin Company, 1961.

Sager, Clifford. *Marriage Contracts and Couple Therapy: Hidden Forces in Intimate Relationships.* New York: Brunner/Mazel, 1976.

Saline, Carol. "How Not to Crumble Under Criticism." *Redbook*, August 1980, p. 19.

Schachter, Stanley, and Singer, J.E. "Cognitive, Social, and Physiological Determinants of Emotional State." *Psychological Review* 69 (1962), pp. 379–399.

Schaefer, Charles, Ph.D. *How to Influence Children: A Handbook of*

Practical Parenting Skills. New York: Van Nostrand Reinhold Company, 1978.

Schroder, Harold M.; Driver, Michael J.; and Streufert, Siegfried. *Human Information Processing.* New York: Holt, Rinehart, and Winston, 1967.

Skinner, B.F. *Science and Human Behavior.* New York: Macmillan Company, 1953.

Sullivan, Harry Stack. *The Interpersonal Theory of Psychiatry.* Edited by Helen Perry and Mary Gawel. New York: W.W. Norton and Company, 1953.

Tavris, Carol. "When to Lie About Sex (And When Not To!)" *Redbook,* October 1978, p. 123.

Taylor, Robert E. "The Effects of Certain Environmental, Organizational, and Psychological Variables Upon the Filtering of Information Inputs by Boundary Role Persons." Doctoral dissertation, University of North Carolina at Chapel Hill, 1974.

Torop, Nancy R. "The Effects of Adult Evaluation on Elementary School Children's Work and Social Interaction: An Experimental Study of Affective Tone and Helpfulness." Doctoral dissertation, Bryn Mawr College, 1973.

"Troublemakers in the Office." *Time,* 17 March 1980, p. 72.

Whitman, Ardis. "The One Person No Woman Forgives." *Woman's Day,* 24 April 1978, p. 74.

Wolpe, Joseph. *Psychotherapy by Reciprocal Inhibition.* Stanford, California: Stanford University Press, 1958.

Zilbergeld, Bernie, and Evans, Michael. "The Inadequacy of Masters and Johnson." *Psychology Today,* August 1980, pp. 29–43.